Perils
and Pearls

In World War II, a Family's Story of Survival and Freedom
from Japanese Jungle Prison Camps

Hulda Bachman-Neeb

Rice paddy field on Island of Flores,
photograph by Peter Neeb

PERILS AND PEARLS: In World War II, a Family's Story of Survival and Freedom from Japanese Jungle Prison Camps
by Hulda Bachman-Neeb

Available for sale on Amazon.com

Published by

BRISTLECONE PRESS
Estes Park, Colorado

Editing: Jen Zelinger, TwinOwlsAuthors.com
Book Design: Nick Zelinger, NZGraphics.com

ISBN: 978-0-578-56744-0 (Soft Cover)
Library of Congress Cataloging in Publication Data

First Edition

Printed in the United States of America

For Jim, my husband

In memory of my mother, Oetie, who twice gave life
to my brother Peter and me

In memory of Grandmother Waldeck
and
Aunts Jette
Kaethe
Louise

who nourished us

For Peter, who shared the same fate,
and his wife, Alja

For the postwar generation:

My brothers
Robbert
Hans

My nieces and nephews and their families:
Laura Hulda, my godchild
Joelle Adrienne
Vanessa Oetie
Friso, my godson
Vincent

So they know

and honoring the courage of my late father,
Dr. Hendrik Neeb

"How ludicrous and outlandish is astonishment at anything that happens in life."

~ Marcus Aurelius (121–180 AD)
Meditations

Table of Contents

Introduction

A while back, I sat down with my mother to ask her about our time as World War II prisoners of Imperial Japan in the Pacific Rim. We are Dutch and spent three and a half years in a Japanese concentration camp. Before we began our session, I wanted to know if talking about these years would be too painful for her. She answered: "It's all right; we need to talk. But not too long, please. We'll do it in stages."

Only she could clarify my memories, and as it was a subject not often mentioned in our house, which intuitively I knew to respect, I had been compiling a list of questions. My mother and I spent many hours recalling the camp years with a sense of relief that they were finally out in the open.

Ever after, my mother became less and less reluctant, and toward the end of her life, she would on occasion spontaneously recall the past, with or without emotion. It may have been a comfort for her, a kind of therapy, to find a good listener in me. After the war, all camp survivors, including my family, did their very best to bury the experience. We had our hopes and expectations for the future; we needed to come to the realization that loved ones, possessions, a carefree life, were lost forever. Unfortunately, not all were equally successful in subduing the traumas and demons and needed psycho-social assistance. Yet, the greater story is the revelation of the strength of the human spirit to transcend injuries and not become victimized by the past.

My own memories consist of a collection of incidents. They are fragmented since I was very young, but my mother's formed a chain, and so she was my best source of information.

Both my brother Peter and I were born on the island of Flores in the Dutch East Indies, now Indonesia, in the town of Endeh. I was born in 1939, Peter in 1941. The Japanese occupied Flores in May 1942. Since early 1942, Japan had invaded most of the nations in Southeast Asia and the Western Pacific. Other than imperial expansion, motivated by the scarcity of metals and petroleum, its scope was the creation of the Greater East Asia Co-Prosperity Sphere. In order to achieve this grandiose goal, Western influence needed to be banned from its freshly conquered Asian territories. Consequently, all non-Asian citizens were separated from the local population to facilitate the indoctrination into Japanese culture. The Italians and Germans were spared, a result of military and diplomatic treaties that bound Italy and Germany to Japan to form the Axis of Power. However, the Co-Prosperity Sphere slogan was no more than a propaganda line, as was proven by the brutal treatment of the captives throughout Asia.

At the time of our imprisonment in May 1942, my mother was twenty-five years old, I was two-and-a-half, my brother Peter not quite one year old. In March 1942, my father, a medical officer in the Netherlands Indies army, together with a handful of other officers, escaped Flores on a pearl schooner to join the Allies in Australia.

We were a large family in the Dutch East Indies; beginning in the mid-1800s we had come from Holland for careers and adventure. Some members of the clan had returned home over the course of time, but those who stayed in the Indies were all interned in camps that were erected everywhere in the archipelago.

My story is a slice of history about World War II in the Pacific and is also intended as a tribute to America and the American forces who gave us our freedom.

It has been seventy-five years since countless lives were disrupted or destroyed, both in Europe and in the Pacific realm. The world that had existed before 1940 was no more. In total, around sixty-five million people found death in World War II. The figures are not clear; several historians say eighty million people perished, but a figure of 2.5 percent of the world population emerges.

Today, the clouds of conflict continue to darken the skies. The loss of freedom is never far away, and that what was wrested from tyranny and oppression, we now take lightly—at our peril. What really are freedom and human rights? Our captors were under no compulsion to make allowances for us. If they did so, it was strictly by choice. They were not restrained by statutes.

A government which protects human freedom must be a government of law, not of man. Here and abroad, the caretaker of liberty can never rest. Most of us would agree that it is a task worth pursuing.

This book draws upon the recollections of family members, past and present, through interviews, letters, and diaries.

Note

A clarification is in order as to how the Dutch use the terminology of Holland, Dutch, the Netherlands, the Netherlanders, and the Low Countries:

These indications are basically interchangeable.

"Dutch" is used as an adjective or to refer to the population.

The Dutch are also called "Netherlanders."

"The Netherlands" is the geographical name, meaning "low countries." Many parts of the country are below sea level, hence the designation: Low Countries.

"Holland," today widely used, is a reference to one of the provinces which made up the Netherlands in the Dutch Golden Age, the seventeenth century, when Holland was the preeminent province with its commerce, fleet, and wealth.

Amsterdam is the capital city of the Netherlands.

The Hague is the seat of the government, courts, embassies, and the royal family.

Photographs and Illustrations

- Nearly all the photographs, as well as the map of the Flores crossing, come from the family archives.

- The photographs of the camp and the guards are from the album *Geillustreerde Atlas van de Japanse Kampen in Nederlands-Indie, 1942-1945. Asia Minor, Purmerend, 2000. (Illustrated Atlas of the Japanese Camps in the Netherlands-Indies, 1942-1945.)*

- The map of the Zone of Captivity is drawn from the book *Prisoners of the Japanese* by Gavan Daws.

- The images of Prince Maurice, Jan Pieterszoon Coen, the VOC logo, and coins are from Google.

1

The Dutch East Indies

*"Man cannot discover new oceans unless he has
the courage to lose sight of the shore."*
~ Christopher Columbus (1451–1506)

During the dry monsoon, the ocean shines brilliantly. It leaps onto the beach with foam cast up high and the fountain of purple and emerald crystals links the earth with the open sky. When the wet monsoon brings the rains, the sea loses its shine and the somber waves crash onto the shore to retreat again toward the horizon where, in the meantime, the sky has turned almost black.

The two seasons create the rhythm of the island. Under the bright sun of the dry monsoon, the shimmering leaves of the palm trees sway gently in the breeze. The local people reflect the motion as they amble along the shady side of the road, shuffling their light sandals. The lazy tempo is matched by the carts that roll by, pulled along by unhurried oxen, unperturbed by their coolie's cries and whips to go faster. In the yards, chickens join in the rhythm, picking grains at their leisure, and ducks waddle around as if they have a purpose. Overhead, laundry billows on gently swinging clotheslines.

The scene changes when the wet monsoon sets in. Animals and house pets go into hiding, and the quiet rhythm is disturbed. People who need to be outdoors scurry through torrential downpours. Protection is often no more than a newspaper held above the head.

Sometimes large umbrellas of gaudy oilpaper, with their peculiar smell of wet resin, are carried off by the winds like giant butterflies. On the narrow roads, flooded most of the time, the ox carts rattle and splash, tended by their anxious handlers, who are aware they can lose their cargo any moment in a ditch concealed by red, muddy water.

Then, when the storms finally move out, the ocean and the trees rock gently back and forth, resting from the attack. Steam swirls up from the roads, and the air is filled with a heady mixture of scents from freshly watered flowers, wet grass, and unfortunately, the dank smell of mud.

A tropical climate has only two seasons, and temperatures range from 70 to 85 degrees Fahrenheit but can climb up to 90 degrees. The sun burns; the heat is scorching. The northwest monsoon is the wet season from December to March with heavy rainstorms and frequent floods; the southeast monsoon is dry and lasts from May until October. In the tropics the sun sets quickly, in less than fifteen minutes, and creates a brief explosion of brilliant orange and red colors. Flora is abundant from the typical frangipani flowering trees, the coconut palm groves, the multicolored cannas, and many other kinds of flowers, often heavily perfumed. Insects are equally abundant, as are lizards, snakes, and snails. The jungle needs year-round warm temperatures and high humidity for its large variety of trees that look alike, but the diversity of the species can amount to dozens per acre.

Flores, the island of my birth, is such a tropical place and is part of the Lesser Sunda Islands, as is Bali, to the east of Java in Indonesia. It is relatively small, with a surface of 5,000 square miles, a width of forty-one miles, and a length of 220 miles. Portuguese traders saw the island first in 1511 and named it Flores after its flowering tree, the flamboya, with its flaming red blooms and fern-like leaves. Today, the population is mostly Roman Catholic, a leftover of the Dominican missionaries who followed the traders. In 1846, the Dutch and Portuguese governments began negotiations, but it was not until 1854 that Flores became part of the Dutch East Indies. It has an amazing array of languages and customs on so small an island; a minimum of six dialects can be identified with some Malay in the mix, and the many villages have their own type of huts and compounds.

Local hut, photograph by Peter Neeb

The island is home to fourteen active volcanos, of which the best known is the 5,377-foot-high Kelimutu, thirty miles to the east of Endeh. It has three volcanic crater lakes, each of a different color. These colors change several times a month, independently, owing to the fact that the lakes have their own specific connection to the activity of the volcano underneath. Even with its typical topography of a volcanic island, eruptions are rare and produce often no more than minor quakes.

In 1938, my parents traveled from Holland to Batavia on the island of Java, which was a return for my father and a new experience for my mother. My father received his orders from the army to report to the island of Flores to take care of its small military barrack, a hospital, and a bunch of tropical diseases and sores.

Local compound, photograph by Peter Neeb

They made their home in Endeh on the south coast. The house was a comfortable bungalow. They had several servants, as was customary in this part of the world: the *kokki* (cook in Malay), the *djongos* (house boy) who swept and mopped, the *kebon* (gardener), and the *babu* (maid), who served as washerwoman and nanny. Their national attire, for both men and women, was the *sarong*, a cotton, batik cloth wrapped around the waist from the ankles up and a *kabaja*, a long-sleeved top that is white, colored, or patterned. As was the habit of the local population in the archipelago, they also chewed their *sirih*, the betel leaf, every day, all day long, which gave them red lips, a red mouth, and black teeth often ground to the gum. With its wonderful propensities of a mild euphoria or perhaps even of an aphrodisiac, these side effects were happily ignored.

Since the island had no electricity, we used kerosene for lighting and operating our Westinghouse refrigerator. The lamps were smelly, with a hissing sound from the air pressure, and cast long shadows across the rooms with shrill, bright light. Every morning the *djongos* refilled all the lamps, clipped the wicks, and wiped the soot off the glass. When one of the volcanoes began to rumble and the grass started its eerie undulation, the servants would run out of the house in a panic, loudly calling out to the dung beetle that they hoped was hiding somewhere, "I am here; I am here." The beetle, they believe, carries the Earth between its legs, and if it is not aware of human presence, could drop the big ball any time into the dark unknown below.

When I was born in November 1939, the monsoon had not yet broken, a time of intense heat. My father returned from his usual round of the island in time to help with my birth. Also at hand were Sister Berneria and Sister Renalda of the neighboring hospital, with whom my mother had developed close friendships. As we owned the only refrigerator on the island, she met with the sisters every day when she brought ice cubes to the nunnery and the hospital. While my mother recovered, the servants ran the house, and before long, tea was served again on the verandah.

Sisters Berneria and Renalda, two more nuns, and the Mother Superior, all five of them trained nurses overseen by my father, ran the hospital with a local housekeeper. The order they belonged to was very strict; they were not supposed to speak except for one hour a day. Their multiple frocks caused an array of rashes in the tropical heat, which compelled my father to write to the Vatican to request that the nuns be allowed to remove a garment or two.

The mission was relatively large with a bishop and several priests who had a faint notion of medicine. Although they were not qualified to practice, some of the friars would leave their post on the local, sturdy ponies and often be gone for months at the time to preach and heal. The nuns taught the local girls and women to sew and weave, also making efforts to school their pupils in the basics of housekeeping and hygiene.

My father, with two or three helpers, toured the island an average of eighteen days a month on horseback for longer stretches or by car when the clinics and the patients were closer to home. For the long stretch, he had extra provisions in his saddlebags and would know where to stay overnight in more or less comfortable lodgings. Although fighting heat and humidity, he rather enjoyed his tours around the island on the narrow trails and uneven paths through the dense jungle. He rode by ravines and waterfalls under a canopy of green leaves, past several volcanos with their colored lakes. He heard the calls of a variety of birds and was surrounded by the constant hum of insects. "It never ceases to feel like a pioneering experience," he used to say.

My father was in charge of the healthcare of the population, and one of his assignments was to fight the tropical ulcer frambesia or yaw, a disease, usually below the knee, also called jungle rot, that affects the skin, the bones, the cartilage. It is a bacterial infection starting as a circular swollen lesion from a cut or a scratch. If the patient is not treated, it causes disfigurement and severe disabilities. Frambesia will take months to heal, but once the patient is affected, it can be latent for up to fifteen years. It occurs in moist, tropical regions and is a highly contagious disease. My father must have received his own immunization, as he would clean the wounds and inoculate those individuals who had been exposed to infected patients. When bones and joints are affected, it becomes extremely painful, and if complications arise, like a thickening of the skin, walking becomes extraordinarily difficult, with the patient developing something like a crablike gait or what is called a crab yaw.

Clinic with family car

The servants, the nuns, the small hospital, my father's tours, and his work at the hospital were part of our world, a safe world with a pleasant routine. The pay was usually in natura; grateful patients dropped off eggs or chickens or a basket of sweet-scented fruits.

Our house had the typical layout of a tropical bungalow.

Endeh bungalow, 1938

During the dry monsoon we used its large verandah more often than the rooms inside, it was a place where the sea breeze would bring relief. My parents furnished it comfortably with rattan chairs, a table or two, and the unavoidable potted palm. The legs of each piece of furniture, both on the verandah and inside the house, stood in tins of soapy water to ward off the white ants. Lunch was usually served inside, where indispensable ceiling fans stirred the air. The kokki prepared either a European menu with potatoes and plain vegetables, according to my mother's instructions, or local dishes of rice, greens, meats, fish. This she did while squatting on the floor, surrounded by several odd, small charcoal burners, using a fan of dried leaves to keep the flames going. It was miraculous what she managed to produce every day with her primitive utensils. She never burnt anything, and the local dishes, with the many spices, their names too hard to remember, never failed to come to their full aromatic potential. After lunch followed the obligatory rest until tea time, which was family time or the occasion to receive visitors, of which there were usually rather few. The local custom dictated that friendly ties were only maintained with basically five families, the so-called upper class of the island, much to my mother's dismay. "That is elitist," she thought.

Before sunset, my father would check on his patients and afterward retire again to the verandah. Together with my mother, he would watch the fiery glow in the sky and the indigo contours of the mountainous volcanos in the background. By then, the *djongos* had lit the kerosene lamps, the crickets would chirp, the geckos would climb the walls, and a last cool drink was served before retiring.

The bedrooms surrounded the living room; it was an open floor plan. The beds were outfitted with mosquito nets and a so-called Dutch wife, a large tube-type pillow to use between the legs to minimize the effects of heat and sweat. On the gallery behind the dining area, we had a bathroom with a cement tub in its corner and a small bucket on the ledge we filled with water to use as a shower.

Further down were the storage room where the supplies were kept, the kitchen, the washing room, the luggage room, and the garage, as well as the servant quarters. Occasionally, one or two of the servants would prefer to stay with the family rather than go home to their village after the day's work. My mother had breakfast served on the verandah in the relative cool of the early morning, and so the day could begin.

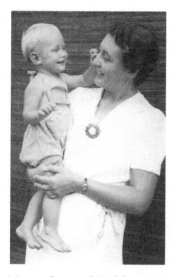

My mother and Hulda, 1940   *My father and Hulda, 1940*

For my father, the Dutch East Indies were familiar territory; for my mother, it was all new and a cultural shock. My father was born in 1912 in Muntok on Bangka, a small island off the east coast of Sumatra. He was a descendant of a prominent Dutch family that left Holland in the 1860s to follow the footsteps of those pioneers who had gone before, as early as the sixteenth century.

Europeans in Southeast Asia, among them the Dutch, came from nations of empire builders who were mainly in search of spices and lucrative business, at the same time looking for new sea routes and unknown territory. It was the age of explorers: James Cook opened the Pacific; Ferdinand Magellan was the first to circumnavigate the globe; Vasco da Gama sailed to Asia; the Dutchman Abel Tasman, in the service of the Vereenigde Oostindische Compagnie, or VOC (United Dutch East Indies Company), explored the oceans (Tasmania, off New Zealand, is named after him) and landed in the Indies, just to name a few of those intrepid navigators. Columbus had sailed earlier, in the fifteenth century.

They were also the first cartographers of maps that were much in need but virtually nonexistent at the time, shaping worldwide geographical knowledge. Jan Pieterszoon Coen (1587-1629) established Batavia on the island of Java in 1619 as an officer of the Vereenigde Oostindische Compagnie, which was founded in 1602 by the States General at the instigation of the statesman Johan van Oldenbarnevelt (1547-1619).

Johan van Oldenbarnevelt
(17th century print)

Even though he had his eye on the advancement of Dutch commerce, van Oldenbarnevelt's main purpose was to inflict losses on the Spanish and Portuguese competitors. The Dutch, traditionally able seafarers, began trade in the Far East in the seventeenth century. Since the merchant fleet had become by far the greatest in the world, van Oldenbarnevelt saw the potential of a Dutch international trading company gaining a dominant position in global business. Initially founded as a worldwide commercial enterprise, before long the States General bestowed on the VOC the instruments of war for the fight on the seas against the powerful Spanish empire and to push out the Portuguese and English.

The company could build its own forts and shipyards, have soldiers and fleets, wage war, and conclude treaties with foreign powers. The VOC became the very first multinational organization because it controlled, or owned even, production of goods in several countries while it minted its own coins. It wielded immense power for two hundred years. However, less successful management between 1720 and 1799 caused the unavoidable decline, and the company was dissolved in 1799. With its demise, its assets were taken by the government, and the VOC's territories became Dutch colonies.

Stadholder, or the chief magistrate, at the time was Prince Maurice of Orange (1567-1625, Maurits van Oranje, in Dutch). The relationship between the prince and van Oldenbarnevelt was a complicated one. The young prince had at first been the protégé of van Oldenbarnevelt, twenty years his senior, the seasoned statesman, counsel to the States General, de facto chief minister of Holland, and Secretary of State. When Maurice came more and more into his own, evolving into a military strategist and winning important field battles as a military organizer and innovator, he also began to show an interest in politics and policies. As the latter had hitherto strictly been the domain of van Oldenbarnevelt, tensions between the two men began to rise, generating into a genuine competition.

As Maurice sought greater power for himself to steer the ship of state, he was looking for a subterfuge to eliminate van Oldenbarnvelt. He found it in a religious dispute. Since over several centuries, religion had been playing, and continued to play, an overwhelming political role in various nations, including the Low Countries, the prince used the opposing views within the Calvinist religion, the main denomination in the Netherlands, as his weapon. It was a conflict between the orthodox Calvinists, who saw themselves as the guardians of the true faith, and a less devout breed. The adversaries of van Oldenbarnevelt accused him of being a free-thinking Calvinist and of secretly sympathizing with the Catholic Church. The campaign of character assassination had begun.

Prince Maurice of Orange

To discredit him, pamphlets were distributed labeling van Oldenbarnevelt as a stalwart Catholic, a perfidious sample of what today we would call "fake news." The straightlaced clergy, by far the most powerful element in Holland, controlling both the church and the people, by now wanted to get rid of van Oldenbarnevelt as well. The prince saw his chance, and so, opportunistically, chose the side of the strict Calvinists. Consequently, van Oldenbarnevelt found himself automatically in the opposition, charged even with treason.

Statue of Johan van Oldenbarnevelt

Today, the power struggle between politics and religion is difficult for modern people to understand. But in that era, the pieces were in play for a deadly game of chess between these two eminent men of state, a game van Oldenbarnevelt ultimately lost. The prince had him arrested and secluded, his estate and inheritance were forfeited. The trial lasted eight months, during which time he was locked up in a small room in one of the buildings of Parliament. He was allowed to retain his valet. May 13, 1619, was the day of the execution of this frail, seventy-one-year-old man, who mounted the scaffold supported by his faithful servant, asking for no more than his nightcap and a quick goodbye. He was decapitated in the courtyard of the Parliament buildings, and so, Maurice was delivered from his political opponent.

Van Oldenbarnevelt's widow was granted a meager pension. The execution remains highly controversial, a black page in the history of the Netherlands. To this day, books have been and are being written about this elder politician, his exploits, his statesmanship, his trial, and his sentence. His relationship with Prince Maurice of Orange has been a source of continuous analysis. Not until both Maurice and van Oldenbarnevelt were adequately rehabilitated was van Oldenbarnevelt rewarded with an imposing statue, situated across from Parliament in The Hague, for his forty-three years of unstinting loyalty and service to the country. May 13, 2019, marks the 400th year of his execution. To commemorate the event, new books and articles in newspapers and historical magazines celebrated Johan van Oldenbarnevelt. During numerous ceremonies in and around The Hague, he was portrayed as the greatest statesman the Netherlands has ever known.

Interestingly, van Oldenbarnevelt's name appears in my family tree, and at a solemn ceremony in 1954 when his statue was unveiled, the queen, several dignitaries, and my grandparents were honored guests. It is a peculiar coincidence that van Oldenbarnevelt, who was so significantly connected with the VOC that drew the Dutch, including my family, to the East Indies, figures among my ancestors.

The VOC traded throughout Asia, the Indies included. Jan Pieterszoon Coen, in its service, reaped many successes on his voyages. Because he had acquitted himself so admirably of his various commissions, in 1618, the directors of the VOC appointed him Governor General of the Dutch East Indies. With nineteen ships he stormed the coast of Java, laid siege to the harbor of Jayakarta, and immediately set out to secure a clove and nutmeg monopoly by fighting the British who owned the rights to the spices. The British finally withdrew. Next came the expulsion of the local forces, and when this was completed, Coen founded Batavia on the ashes of Jayakarta and declared it the capital. Batavia, today's Jakarta, became the central headquarters of the VOC in the Indies; Amsterdam was its seat in Holland.

Jan Pieterszoon Coen

It goes without saying that these conquests did not occur without plenty of cannonades and bloodshed, turning Coen into a controversial figure with the reputation of a ruthless warrior. Nevertheless, the colonies in the Indies continued to thrive, as did the other overseas possessions, and during the two centuries of the VOC's existence, they provided considerable fortunes and goods for the Dutch Republic. From this enormous wealth rose the Dutch Golden Age, the rich seventeenth century, with its incomparable art and architecture.

In Holland, the colonies were gaining in popularity as a result of the accounts of the returning seafarers, whose enthusiasm and confidence in the Indies were a source of inspiration. Returning civil servants penned their memoirs or gave lectures, although not all of these were positive as voices would arise denouncing the Dutch presence as abusive colonialism. Yet, this could not put a damper on the excitement of a promising career in the exotic realms of the tropics, overseas prospects became more and more enticing. Consequently, in the early nineteenth century, the government established several educational facilities for the training of civil servants in the Dutch East Indies.

This is how my grandmother's father, Charles Rene Bakhuizen van den Brink (1850-1923), came to the Indies to forge a career for himself. His father had died when Charles Rene was young, and although Bakhuizen Sr. was an illustrious author and literary critic in the Netherlands, the means for a continued study for Charles Rene were short.

Upon the advice of well-meaning relatives and friends of his father's and under the spell of the many authors who had written positively about the colonies, he decided to prepare himself for the East Indies. He passed the obligatory exams, and so, as a newly minted civil servant, Charles Rene sailed for the colonies. He arrived in 1870 in Batavia, the seat of government, and received an appointment as a clerk at the Department of Finance, where he would remain for the next thirty years, ultimately becoming its director.

He went steadily up the ladder, not in the least because of his deep-seated interest in the culture and customs of the country and its people. He spoke Malay fluently and later in life was recognized for his devotion and knowledge with several honors and decorations. The Governor General then appointed him Resident of Batavia in 1901, a position he held until he returned to Holland in 1906.

The Resident was a highly placed government official. For the sake of an accessible control system, the East Indies were divided into three provinces that were again divided into *residenties* (departments); each of these departments could well be three times larger than the size of the Netherlands. West Java had five *residenties* of which Batavia was one of considerable importance.

The Resident, as the representative of the Governor General in his district and in his function as chief commissioner of police, was responsible for law and order in the area. A considerable part of his duties consisted of supervising the administrative machinery in his extensive department. This enabled Charles Rene, committed to traveling all over his sizeable territory, to satisfy his curiosity in regard to the way of life of the local inhabitants.

Charles Rene Bakhuizen van den Brink and his wife Henriette

In 1878, he married twenty-year-old Henriette Raedt van Olden-barnevelt, born and raised in the East Indies. They had five children, one son and four daughters, of whom my father's mother was one, the eldest born in 1879.

Grandmother Louisa ("Loekie" for the family) and her four siblings were raised in all the comforts that came with their father's position. As director of the Department of Finance, Charles Rene had at his disposal a large house with the mandatory verandah and its columns, surrounded by ample grounds. Several servants took care of the family and the property.

Young Grandmama

The official home after his appointment as Resident of Batavia offered even larger accommodations with wider verandahs, taller and additional white columns, and more potted plants. Every day, the grounds and the flowerbeds were tended by several prisoners and their guard from the nearby jail.

In the meantime, the East Indies had continued to modernize its cities; important irrigation systems were laid out, transportation arteries such as railways and canals, as well as an extensive network of roads, were engineered. Many research stations began experimenting in the field of mining, agriculture, fishing, forestry. Educational institutions flourished in vocational training or veterinary science. Elementary and high schools were established, as well as medical colleges, law schools, and technical institutes. For the development of the colonies, doctors, engineers, teachers, and scientists arrived in full force from the Netherlands.

Their presence went hand-in-hand with a need for entertainment after the long days of strenuous work in the heat of the sun or in sultry department offices that, in turn, gave cultural life a big boost. Local performers created theater groups and musical evening events, sometimes with artists from the Netherlands; many libraries saw the light of day; clubhouses and pavilions with amply equipped liquor bars became favorite resorts, and sports like tennis and soccer thrived. Social life developed along the lines of the etiquette of the day, mysterious as its rules were regarding their origin. Visiting cards and courtesy calls were properly exchanged. Ladies and girls dressed elegantly, often in white muslin, the bodices of the dresses tightly adorned with ruffles at the wrist and neck, with skirts flowing. Men suffered the tropical temperatures in their suits with high, stiff shirt collars.

Row of guests

The lives of Charles Rene and Henriette, together with their children, went along the required paths of their comfortable station.

For Grandmother Loekie this changed radically when she married Grandfather Evert (Everardus Adrianus Neeb, 1869-1960), also born and raised in the Dutch East Indies. The year of the wedding was 1899. My grandmother was eighteen years old, her husband ten years her senior.

Wedding Grandmama and Grandpapa Neeb

My grandfather's profession as a mining engineer took him to the tin mines of the island of Bangka, a remote place far from the civilization my grandmother had known and enjoyed. My grandfather was a severe man, ramrod and principled, my grandmother, young and vivacious, and at her eighteen years an ingenue. They settled in the main town, Muntok, and here, my grandmother's woes began.

She felt lonely, she was upset with her eventless life, and it did not take her long before she developed an overwhelming desire to leave the island to go home to Batavia. She responded to her impulses and loaded a cart with a suitcase packed by her *babu* with some clothes and toiletry articles. She gathered pots and pans and large kettles with water. Once satisfied she had everything for her journey, she fetched a horse and, with deafening clanging of the ill-arranged cookware, she and the *babu* left the compound.

The *djongos* had run as fast as he could to find my grandfather to warn him, but my grandfather remained unfazed. He knew the island like the palm of his hand and quickly calculated that my grandmother would be home again at dinner time. Besides, he also knew that she was afraid of the dark, and especially of darkness in a jungle with its creepy noises of the night.

Indeed, my grandmother did return at dusk, and not a word about her little excursion was spoken at the dinner table. Yet somehow, she had the fixed notion that she had taken the wrong route, the distressed *babu* useless as a guide, and that somewhere out there was the path that would take her off the island. She had no idea how to return to Batavia, but her foremost desire was to get away. And so, she set out on her journey once or twice more, always home again at the dinner hour.

In time, she adjusted to the slow pace of the island; she had no choice, and learned to accept its inconveniences and hardships. Then the children were born, first Evert in 1900, followed by Louise ("Dee") in 1902, and ten years later came Hendrik ("Henk"), my father, in 1912. Although his base was Muntok, my grandfather often traveled around the archipelago, with or without my grandmother and his family, to take stock of mineral resources. Occasionally, he needed to go to China to recruit laborers for the tin mines. Once, his travels took him to Siam, today's Thailand, on a gold expedition. As a tourist, he visited Tibet, where he picked up several souvenirs, silk, jade, and a smattering of yoga.

Family in Muntok

Grandfather Evert Neeb was a scion of a family with roots in Leyden that had won its spurs as surgeons. A certain Johan Philippus Neeb (1767-1840) served as the official surgeon of the town, as did his son Jan Frederik (1797-1873). The trend continued, with this difference that the following generations enlisted as officers of health in the Dutch East Indies Army. Grandfather Evert's father, Pieter (1830-1902), a physician, was the first to relocate to the Indies while enlisting in the army. He was married twice, losing his first wife and two children at a young age during a cholera epidemic. One son survived, Christiaan. With his second wife, Pieter had nine children. His career must have gone well since he was the recipient of multiple decorations from the Netherlands Government.

Christiaan (1860-1924), another physician in the family as well as an army officer of health, proved to be very musically inclined. He had a grand piano shipped to him from Holland, which required fortifications of his home with extra foundation and piling. In his spare time, he composed; one of his songs in honor of his Leyden fraternity is still performed today. His appointment as army photographer resulted in an album that is archived in the Royal Tropical Institute in Amsterdam. He had a daughter, Annie, who perished in one of the Japanese concentration camps.

Henri (1870-1933) was one of the sons of Pieter's second marriage, one more physician, one more army officer of health, one more family member with an impressive career who was highly decorated. The appointed inspector general of the Dutch East Indies Army's Health Department, he became a professor at the Technical High School in Bandung, which later became the first established university in the Indies. The army officially appointed Henri also its photographer, and a collection of his photographs is archived at the University of Leyden as well as at the Royal Tropical Institute in Amsterdam, like his brother Christiaan's.

Grandfather Evert, another son among the nine children of Pieter's second marriage, broke the chain by studying mining at the Technical University in Delft and worked as the Head engineer of the Bangka-Billiton Tin Company that later became a subsidiary of Shell.

Mine engineers in the tropics retire at the age of fifty-five, and when the year 1924 came around, it was time for the family to relocate to the Netherlands. Since Bangka did not provide the best schooling, the two older children, Evert and Dee, had gone ahead to Holland to live with their grandparents, Bakhuizen van den Brink, who had left Batavia in 1906 upon the completion of Charles Rene's duties as Resident. My father, as a twelve-year-old boy, came with his parents to The Hague to finish his schooling. Faithful to tradition, he enrolled at the University of Leyden to study medicine; his ancestors, his grandfather, his uncles had all been students of this illustrious institution.

For my father and his parents, the change from the sweltering tropics, the verdant scenery and the variety of flora and fauna, to the mild maritime world of the Netherlands required major adjustments, in both climate and living patterns. Still, regardless of how well they adapted, their yearning for the tropics remained undiminished.

2

Beginnings in Holland

*"It is a mistake to look too far ahead. Only one link of
the chain of destiny can be handled at a time."*
~ Winston Churchill (1874-1965)

When my mother, Oetie (Theodora Wilhelmina Hulda Waldeck),
was twelve years old, no such demands for adjustments were
made on her. These came later.

My mother was privileged to be raised in a quiet village near The
Hague in an attractive historical house on a canal named Vliet.

*Old postcard of the ancestral home
"In de Werelt is veel Gevaer"*

It is a stately mansion, built in 1793 by Abraham Nau, who descended from Huguenot refugees hailing from France. The building style is Louis XVI, and quite remarkable are the Palladian pediment, the triangle above the main entrance with a garland on both sides of the oculus, and the two large chimneys. People named houses in the eighteenth century, and the family Nau titled this one "In de Werelt is veel Gevaer" inscribed, in old-Dutch spelling, on the frame of the front door facing the canal. The meaning of *gevaer* is twofold: peril and navigation. Translated it says: "The World knows many Perils" or "There is much Navigation in the World." The name and its implications are very Dutch, as the warning of the "perils" reflect the pessimistic Protestant nature, whereas "navigation" is a business the Dutch were well acquainted with. For short, the house was also called the Vliethuis (house) after the canal.

The Waldeck family arrived in Holland from Germany in 1883: father, mother, and four children.

Schloss Waldeck am Edersee, Great-Grandpapa's origins

Count Friedrich Wilhelm Christiaan Waldeck owned a paint factory in Bonn, but due to health issues caused by the paint fumes, he abandoned his business and found different employment elsewhere. His choice was Holland and the town of Voorburg, near the city of The Hague, though his occupation at the time is unclear. The Vliethuis had known several occupants before Great-Grandfather Waldeck purchased it in 1911.

Great-Grandfather Count Friedrich Wilhelm Waldeck

In 1909, the son Friedrich and Theodora are married.

Wedding of my Grandparents,
Friedrich Waldeck and Theodora van Cappellen, 1909

After he had bought the Vliethuis, he transformed the annexes, which had been used as a boarding school for boys by the previous owner, into a large steam laundry facility in which he put to work his four children, my grandfather, and his three sisters, as well as men and women from the surrounding village. Some of his laborers occupied small houses in a narrow street nearby. He began his business with horse-drawn wagons to attend to his customers, but naturally, upgraded his fleet to motorized transportation as soon as it became available, and especially, practical.

When Count Friedrich Wilhelm moved his family to the house on the canal, there were eight: himself, his wife Hulda, after whom my mother and I are named, the three daughters and the son (Friedrich) with his wife (Theodora) and child, their firstborn, my mother's brother Frits. The daughters were my dear great-aunties, the son was my mother's father.

*Grandfather and Grandmother Waldeck around the time
they moved into the Vliethuis*

The aunts, Jette, Kaethe, and Louise, three beautiful women, never married; their father was a stern Prussian and needed them in his business. Upon his death, the enterprise stayed in the family, the aunts participating until the end of their days.

Aunt Louise was engaged to be married for twelve years, the dowry of linens, towels, china, silver, growing over time. Her father would not consent to the marriage, hoping that it would blow over—which it eventually did. Aunts Jette and Kaethe did not get further with their suitors than a cup of tea in the drawing room, their father always close by. Some callers never made it beyond the front door, with Kaethe and Jette waiting inside, anxiously looking at the clock as the hour of the rendezvous came and went.

At times, the aunts adorned their throats with velvet chokers, plain during the week, and on Sundays, they wore others embroidered with colored beads or pearls. Sundays were special, dedicated for the most part to the entertainment of my mother and her brother. They were taken to the pier of Scheveningen near The Hague for a healthy walk in the morning and around the Vliet canal in the afternoon. When the Russian Cossack Choir was in town, that is in The Hague, they never missed a performance to introduce my mother and Frits to the beauty and benefits of good music, insisting they dress up for the occasion. Being childless, they lavished their love upon their niece and nephew, the same unqualified affection my brother Peter and I would experience many, many years later.

Aunts and Frits in living room

The front of the mansion facing the canal had thirteen tall windows, the outside shutters were louvered, inside they were paneled; the windows on the ground floor consisted of nine lights in the upper sash and sixteen in the lower one. The ceilings were of an impressive height.

The aunts lived in their own wing of the house, complete with a sitting room, kitchen, and dining room, and separated by a glass door, the rest of the family was well accommodated on the other side. In the central hall stood a heavy brass gong suspended on wooden legs; every stroke with the drumstick and a combination of strokes communicated its own message for each person, wherever in the house. Wide marble corridors connected the rooms and a number of staircases. Steam from the laundry heated the house, pushed through a multitude of pipes; lighting was by gas until the advent of electricity in the 1920s. Telephone service became available around that time as well.

My mother was born in 1916; Frits in 1911. Their brother Marius, born in 1913, drowned in the canal in 1918 while feeding ducks. The grief over the loss of the little boy lessened over time but was always present in the faces of his loved ones. It was the saddest event in my mother's childhood, a childhood that was otherwise cheerful and harmonious.

My mother and Frits grew up with a quiet, warm, and affectionate father who had an easy sense of humor. Their mother used to welcome family and her children's friends with unflagging hospitality. There were always guests for dinner or tea and many musical evenings were arranged; classical music was part of life. My mother took singing and piano lessons. When phonograph records appeared around the 1910s, the family became avid collectors, listening to the still-scratchy reproductions when not attending concerts in The Hague. The pianists Moura Lympany, or Paderewski and Rachmaninoff, who played their own compositions; the singers Galli-Curci, Pinza, Gigli, the violinist Heifetz became household names. When the conductor and composer Peter van Anrooy came to the Vliethuis for dinner, my mother was transfixed by the facility with which he read the music score he had brought with him, humming and beating time with his hands or feet. He wrote musical notes as if writing a letter and would read the score, rapidly turning pages, like a book.

My mother's engagement photograph

My mother finished schooling, and having a green thumb, acquired a certificate in landscaping, at the same time continuing her musical education. Frits chaperoned her to balls and dances, a favorite pastime in the nineteen-twenties and -thirties. By that time my father had found his footing in Holland. As a medical student at the University of Leyden he had made friends with whom he did a lot of sailing and rowing on the numerous lakes and canals, winning many prizes.

The town of Leyden is full of history. In part, it is well-known as the departure scene in 1620 of the Pilgrims to the American colonies. The university, founded in 1575, established the first botanical gardens behind the buildings for the benefit of the medical students, the "Hortus Botanicus," the oldest in the world. The prefect of the gardens kept in touch with the VOC to obtain tropical specimens for research. The famous botanist was Boerhaeve (1688-1738) before Linnaeus expanded the gardens in 1736. The *hortus* has been, and continues to be, cultivated as an object of scientific development and is open to the public.

My parents, engaged

After a study of seven years my father received his degree in medicine from this prestigious institution. The Netherlands Army swore him in as a medical officer, having born part of the cost of his studies on condition that he return the favor by being in its service in the Dutch East Indies for a period of ten years. He began his career as First Lieutenant, with promotions further down the road.

My parents getting married on a windy day, 1938

Because they moved in the same circles in and around The Hague, it was virtually inevitable that the paths of Oetie and Hendrik would cross. And so they did; at one of the balls, my parents met in 1934. They were married in 1938, at that time, my mother was twenty-two years old and my father was twenty-six.

My mother never questioned how her circumstances would change; getting married to my father was the important issue and the contours of life beyond were vague, although she was aware of my father's feelings for the East Indies and his desire to return to the country of his childhood. When it began to dawn on her that her departure from the Vliethuis became unavoidable, she decided to get an education at the "Colonial School," as it was called, in The Hague. Her brief time there scraped off some of her ignorance about her new home, but between a few words of Malay and my father's memories, she was not very well prepared for the radical change in her life.

In July of 1938, my parents sailed for the Indies, on a ship (was it by chance?) named *Oldenbarnevelt*, a journey that took three weeks. My father's siblings, Evert and Dee, welcomed them in Batavia. They had returned to the Indies immediately after they completed their studies. Both were married with children and lived a distance away from Batavia in the hills of Bandung.

Family in Batavia, 1938; Dee and Gerard, my mother, Evert, and my father; Gerard and my father in their uniform of health officer

Batavia only served as a stopover for my parents while my father awaited his marching orders from the military. My mother felt home-sick and was depressed. The transition from Holland to the tropics proved a huge cultural shock. For my father, on the other hand, it was a reunion with family and old school friends, but especially with memories. "Come here and smell it. I have come home!" he called to my mother when the ship anchored at Batavia's port. For my mother, there was no such elation.

What helped her in the time ahead was her fascination with nature. The visits by car to their relatives in Bandung took my parents six hours on winding mountain roads through abundant vegetation, shimmering in the brightness of the tropical sun. It was full of wonder, my mother thought. She admired the rice paddies, stretching toward the blue mountains on the distant horizon, upon the mirror of its shallow water the reflection of clouds and coconut palms. All around her were smells and fragrances that were unfamiliar to her. She began to look forward to more of this beauty.

It was six months before my parents finally sailed from Batavia for the island of Flores. My father carried his instructions in his pocket, and my mother was strengthened by the good counsel of her experienced in-laws. They set up house in the bungalow provided for them by the government on the Bay of Endeh, close to the ocean and the beach, which to my mother's surprise consisted of black volcanic sand and did not look very inviting. My father was in his element; my mother learned new things every day. She paid calls to the few families, all in one government service or another, that had already established themselves, received more counsel, and made friends with the nuns of the hospital and the nunnery.

When I was born in November 1939, her daily routine took on a different dimension. The frequent letters with many photographs to the Vliethuis contained happier descriptions, and her observations suggested a keener interest in her environment.

Then, suddenly, about six months later, all of this   collapsed when communication with Holland fell silent; the letters back and forth stopped.

It was war in Europe. After Hitler's Luftwaffe (air force) heavily bombed the city of Rotterdam as a warning, the German invasion immediately followed. The Dutch government capitulated on May 10, 1940. At this point, France, Norway, and Denmark had already been invaded by Hitler's armies, together with Poland in 1939. What news was getting through from the European scene was erratic, to say the least. On top of the lack of information from the homeland, the fate of her family caused my mother great anxiety. When Peter was born in June 1941, my parents sent a telegram with the announcement, but they learned later that it never reached the Vliethuis.

Still, the war in Europe was far away, geographically and philo-sophically, the proof of which was the visit of Grandpapa and Grandmama Neeb to Endeh in 1941. Since Grandfather Evert's retirement in 1924, they had been living in The Hague, but the Dutch Indies continued to exert its pull, and in 1939, my grandparents left Holland for Java to be with their sons and daughter and their families. Even though the clouds were gathering, and reports from Germany became increasingly troubling, the possibility of a war in the Pacific never crossed their mind, and so they went ahead with their plans. They lived in Java for a year before they arrived in Endeh in August of 1941, a few months after the birth of their grandson Peter.

Besides visiting family, my grandpapa had an itinerary, he was an organizer and never left anything to chance. On the Endeh schedule figured an excursion to the island of Komodo, just off the coast of Flores, a trip of three hours by boat. The island was, and still is,

Endeh, August, 1941

known for its dragons, the largest living monitor lizard that can be long as nine feet, weighing about 200 pounds. Today there are still some 4,000 of them left in the world. It is a most lugubrious, fearsome creature, crawling over the island, a tourist attraction then and today.

As if that expedition was not enough, my grandpapa's next jaunt aimed at visiting a tribe in the south of the island of Celebes, Sulawesi today, the Toradjas, a trip of fourteen days and fourteen hundred miles. On October 1, 1941, my grandparents arrived in Macassar, a town that would play a sad role in our lives just a few months later. They used the Grand Hotel as their base for two months.

It was the funeral rites of the Toradja tribe, involving buffalo skulls and lasting several days, that had intrigued my grandfather. As he was an enthusiastic photographer, the family possesses numerous pictures of burial sites in rocky cliffs, of natives, of tribal dwellings, of woodcarvings and other artifacts. We have his diary, in which he cataloged his impressions with the utmost precision and extensive descriptions, typed or written in longhand.

Before setting out on their trip, my grandparents, although my grandmama admittedly not half as enamored, spent long hours in their hotel suite studying the ethnic identity of the tribe, its history, the makeup of its society, and as aspiring anthropologists, armed with a fair knowledge of the people, they toured the Toradja land for two weeks in a rented car with a driver.

When they returned to Endeh, it was December 1, 1941.

3

War Hits Home

"War is the greatest plague that can afflict humanity,
it destroys religion, it destroys states, it destroys families.
Any scourge is preferable to it."
~ Martin Luther (1483-1546)

While up-country on the island of Celebes, my grandparents remained unaware of the looming disaster about to befall the entire Pacific Rim and East Asia. When they arrived back in Endeh, they were surprised to find my father and mother deeply worried, insisting they leave the island immediately because of the disconcerting rumors they had picked up from the radio. My grandparents left on the last boat from Flores to Java before the Japanese raid on Hawaii's Pearl Harbor on December 7, 1941.

Even though the surprise attack on the United States was still a few days away, the relay station in Batavia broadcasted the ominous Tripartite Alliance between Japan, Germany, and Italy to the islands of the archipelago, accompanied by somber commentary. The Axis carried with it the seeds of all-out war, a world war. Germany's successful occupation of one nation after another on the European continent gave the Alliance a boost and Japan an incentive. Japan realized that Germany's rapid advances worked to its advantage; it looked strong and invincible, and so Japan proceeded to form a defensive alliance with Adolf Hitler, the Tokyo-Berlin Axis, which promised to come to each other's aid if one of them was attacked.

War came ever closer.

It may have been a surprise attack on Hawaii's harbor, and for that matter on Hong Kong, Shanghai, on the islands of Guam and Wake the very same day, but it was by no means an invasion, and thus a declaration of war, that had not been carefully prepared by Japan for more than ten years. To begin with, the Japanese Consulate on Hawaii was a nest of spies; valuable information was transmitted to Tokyo by secret code. Hawaii's harbor with a great part of the American fleet on anchor was an accident waiting to happen.

Furthermore, since the founding of the empire 2,600 years ago, Japan had adhered to the philosophy that the world should be one big family with unfailing loyalty to the emperor. Thus, there was no avoiding the creation of a Greater East Asia Co-Prosperity Sphere, which naturally involved grabbing oil, minerals, rubber, and other raw materials wherever they were available. Japan began its outward thrust in 1931, when it moved into Manchuria, Korea, and China. By then it had become evident that the strife between the military and the government was tilting in favor of the military, yet with "Emperor worship" as a unifying symbol.

Manchuria and China were good training grounds for the army and navy. Even though Japan advertised itself as the liberator of the colored peoples of Asia from the yoke of the hated white Europeans, it committed the most hideous brutality, torturing and slaughtering countless thousands of civilians, using many of their victims for bayonet practice. Occupying Manchuria by force, they believed they had a right to do so as the "Master Race of the East," identical to Hitler's "Herrenvolk" theory. They established a government run by the military. In 1937, Peking and Shanghai fell and finally Nanking. The fall of Nanking, the capital of the new Republic of China, is described by Iris Chang in her book *The Rape of Nanking,* with as its subtitle, "The Forgotten Holocaust of World War II." The book is a disturbing chronicle of indescribable atrocities carried out by the Japanese soldiers in Nanking and elsewhere in China. Because Japan left the League of Nations in 1920 and had not ratified the Geneva Convention regarding the treatment of prisoners of war either, it was not subjected to any international, annoying, supervision, with all the consequences for its victims, accountability had gone out the window.

Imperial Japan continued to pull the wool over the eyes of the United States, trying on all fronts not to raise suspicion about its war-like activities, pretending to be a peaceful power, even though its actions in China were well-known. Through the intermediary of the Japanese ambassador to Washington, the two nations repeatedly introduced bills and treaties that were totally unacceptable and only intended to keep the United States off balance. This charade by the two envoys from Japan, the Ambassadors Nomura and Kurusu, to fool the American Secretary of State Cordell Hull and the American government, continued well into the last hour, when the Pacific war had already begun. (A similar deception would doubtlessly be impossible today with the advanced electronic communications systems.)

All the while, this cleverly devised smokescreen hid the preparatory movements of the army and navy during the "War Games" at the Navy War College in Tokyo and the training of the Samurai in the Bushido code with its specific warrior techniques. The War College handed out to the trainees explicit manuals as to how to kill best, how to torture, how to fine-tune the art of humiliation, and how to perform a swift decapitation. The latter was the favorite mode of execution. However, the Samurai received instruction in other methods as well, such as deadly beatings, burning, drowning, and kicking. Often, they used prisoners for target drills; they became accomplished torturers.

The Bushido warrior code, same as the ideology that "the world is one big family," also goes back centuries. In the name of the emperor, Samurai would fight to the death. Japan's warriors would never show their backs to the enemy, and they were imbued with total and utter contempt for military prisoners of war. In their minds, these soldiers had succumbed to the cowardly act of surrender, which was the thinking behind the horrible treatment in the camps, in the hulls of the slave ships bound for Japan, on the death marches.

Because of the surprise element of the Japanese attacks, America was ill-prepared for war. However, not long after the events in Pearl Harbor and elsewhere in the Pacific Rim, peacetime industries converted to military production with astounding results and, in no time, America was able to provide war matériel whenever and wherever it was needed. As a by-product, but not an insignificant one, the depression in the United States that had started in 1929, was eliminated since manpower was in huge demand; there were jobs for everybody, men and women, and young men were drafted into the military. By the early 1940s, the war production had fully wiped out the Depression.

The Japanese Admiralty received the news of the attack on Pearl Harbor, however much anticipated, with mixed feelings. "It is scary because now we have awakened the sleeping giant."

The ideology of the East Asia Co-Prosperity Sphere, calling for the seclusion of the white people from nefarious "un-Japanese" influences, was a trick, of course. Immediately upon occupying the nations of the Pacific Rim, Japan went to work taking the whites into captivity, posing as the liberator of yellow and brown people from white imperialism, European and American. All non-Asian influence needed to be banned. The camps served as pure and simple prisons. However, in order to set an example, Japanese soldiers did not shy away from massacring local people they suspected of being in league with the enemy. Japan planned to reshape the Pacific realm into a Japanese lagoon with puppet governments and a complete control of trade.

Our fate was yet unknown to us on December 7, 1941.

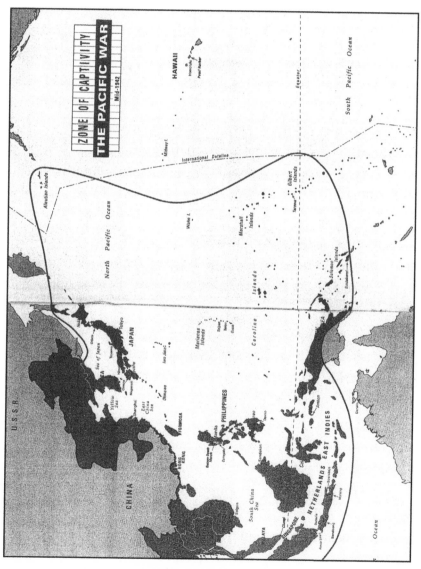

War Map of the Pacific Rim

The invasion by Japan of the Dutch East Indies began on January 10, 1942. It was still relatively quiet on Flores between December 7 and January 10 as war had not yet reached its shores. Yet, that changed quickly. Japanese soldiers roved all over the archipelago, emboldened by their defeat of the Combined Striking Force, the main Allied naval force, in the Java Sea on February 27, a battle that lasted a mere seven hours. Japan's heavy cruisers were much more powerful, armed with big guns and superb torpedoes, than the relatively small Allied force. Again, Japan had prepared itself to the hilt for the invasion and the conquest of new territory, wholly ready to go to war.

My father received a message from long-distance runners when on tour, holding clinic in a far-out village, to return to Endeh immediately and to start mobilization procedures. These began with a few halfhearted attempts, such as the perfunctory internment of one or two German missionaries. But as the advance of the Japanese continued and the islands fell like dominoes, Endeh began to stir. Mobilization began in earnest and people started to move away from the coastal areas into the mountains.

My father's military detachment was to be transferred to Koepang on the island of Timor, as a precautionary measure to prevent the Japanese from using the airports as a jumping-off board for planes to Australia. In view of their pending move, my parents sold their furniture and possessions. They took the memorabilia, family keepsakes from the Vliethuis, wedding presents, silver flatware, and china to the mission post for safekeeping, which turned out to be an illusion. Because their bungalow sat empty, their servants escaped to the villages, my father, my mother, Peter, and I stayed at the hospital, awaiting further instructions from the army commandant.

In the early morning of January 29, 1942, my father's birthday, a ship appeared on the horizon, coming to take my father and his small army detachment to Timor. Originally my father wished to take his wife and children with him to Koepang but realized he would be taking them into a war zone; why else would he be transferred to Timor? So he decided against it. As a soldier, he had no choice; he had to follow orders.

As the ship left the jetty, my father had grave misgivings as he watched his family grow smaller and smaller. What would the future hold? Oetie was twenty-five years old with two small children, a baby of eight months and a toddler of not yet two-and-a-half. It had been difficult enough for her to settle into the Dutch East Indies. Now she was faced with uncertainty, possibly war, and with the separation from her husband after just a little over three and a half years of marriage. When they returned to Endeh from the jetty, what would happen to her and the children, even in the next hour?

As it was, my mother went back to the empty bungalow, borrowed a few pieces of furniture, and sent word to the *babu* to return and assist her. Even though the march of the Japanese through the islands continued unabated, the armies had not yet reached Flores. But word had gone ahead that arrests, shootings, and concentration camps were the order of the day. Tensions among the people of Flores ran high. When would it be its turn to be invaded, and then, what would happen?

My mother felt unsafe on the coast and took her children up-country in mid-February to stay with the Assistant Resident. Yet, when news reached Flores that Java had surrendered on March 1, they all knew that it was only a matter of time before the Japanese would arrive on the island. It was a period of great anguish, as there was nothing to do but wait in fear for events to unfold.

In May 1942, the Japanese landed on Flores.

In the meantime, my father had returned to Endeh from Timor. It was war on Timor. From Flores, his detachment now hoped to reach Java. The Japanese bombed Koepang constantly. They had landed on February 19, 1942, in the south, which was Netherlands Timor, and on Dilly in the north, which was Portuguese. The bombing created pandemonium.

My father and his men did not know what happened to their unit elsewhere on the island. Koepang became a deserted town, parts of it in flames. The population had fled, and only the medical staff remained: two doctors and six nurses. They finally packed up as well and left town in the one remaining ambulance.

They were surrounded by Japanese forces and had to be very artful to avoid capture. Somehow, they figured out where the obstacles were and managed to safely reach port where, much to their relief, they saw a forgotten *prahu*, a local fishing boat. They squeezed in and sailed all night, watching out for the Japanese battle lines. Early in the morning, they landed on a miraculously still unoccupied strip of land and walked to a *kampong* (village), where they rented one or two mules.

Riding and walking, it took them a full day to reach their goal: the Australian hospital located in a small town in the center of the island. My father was in good health. The other doctor, Doctor Hekking, had suffered a malaria attack and was still very weak, but persevered admirably. The ladies were doing fine, but the male nurse was a nuisance, the last thing one needs on an exhausting, anxious trek. Not suffering from any ailment, he complained constantly about the personal discomforts that they all suffered, naturally, but which all of them bore stoically. They wished to give him a good shaking but were afraid of more lamentations. Doctor Hekking, ill as he was, offered the nurse his mule to shut him up since all the negativity was beginning to draw energy out of the group.

When they finally arrived at the Australian hospital, they received word that part of their unit had not been able to get through the Japanese lines and was captured. The lucky circumstance of sailing through the night in a forgotten *prahu* had saved them from a similar fate.

There was no time to lose, as the Japanese were advancing relentlessly. At the hospital, my father was directed to go inland together with the soldiers who had recovered and the medics from Koepang. He learned later that those soldiers too ill to travel had been captured, among them Doctor Hekking, who had made it to the hospital, sick with a renewed bout of malaria, only to be caught.

The journey took my father and the others to the town of Atamboea in the center of Timor, which had not been invaded as yet. It was an arduous trip through a steamy jungle and along overgrown trails, but not in any way comparable to what was still in store for them. They arrived at Atamboea, exhausted, limping into a hut to find a place to sleep after marching day and night, with little or no rest and the Japs on their heels.

At Atamboea, the group split. The Dutch and Australian commandants gave the soldiers permission to leave the island altogether or move on to the areas that had not been taken at that time to save their skin. Timor was lost. The troops disbanded; they were on their own. My father lost sight of the nurses of Koepang. One day, he found Doctor Hekking's name, whom he had to leave behind at the Australian hospital, on a list of a prisoners of war camp in Thailand, together with the name of Doctor Kloosterhuis, his brother-in-law.

It was March 1, 1942. At Atamboea, my father, and the soldiers that were left of his detachment: Lieutenant Stoll, Sergeant de Maar, who was originally from South Africa, and Sergeant Meyer made the decision to try to reach Java from Flores. Stoll had arrived from Dilly, where it had become hopeless to defend the Portuguese section of the island, de Maar had been able to get through the Japanese barricades in Koepang on a motorcycle, and Meyer was up-country when the Japanese landed, searching for a secret transmitter. These men, fugitives from sure captivity, were destined to remain together for several weeks, always on the run.

As the Japanese came dangerously close to their planned northern escape route, the shortest way to the coast, the four of them needed to revise their strategy. They opted for Wini, another coastal town but further away. They got hold of a motorcycle with side-car, piled themselves in, and backtracked on the main road to Koepang toward a town called Kefannanoe, which they found practically deserted, as the Japs had been signaled ominously close.

They continued north toward Wini, a stretch that did not go so well. After only a few miles, they met with one drawback after another, and the previous trip from Koepang to Atamboea began to look like a mere bagatelle. The countryside to the coast was mountainous and forbidding, the locals had destroyed several bridges to prevent the advancing Japanese from crossing, the roads were in a deplorable condition, and the motorcycle began to huff and puff. On top of this, they needed to play hide and seek with the Japanese, who were making impressive inroads. At times, the local population signaled them as close as twenty miles.

When the men learned that many more bridges had been destroyed, it was the last straw. They could not drive any further. They bartered two packing mules against some military equipment, destroyed the motorcycle, and continued on foot. It was eight o'clock in the evening, and they had been on the road since noon. My father and his companions disguised themselves as natives as best they could, which could not have been very successful when tall, pale Caucasians don *sarong* and *kabaja*, but it must have given them a sense of security that their tell-tale uniforms were tucked away in their backpacks. If the Japs should come too close for comfort, all they would see is Timorese milling about, or so the party wishfully thought.

They walked through the night, resting occasionally, and twelve hours later, after thirty miles without unfortunate incidents, they reached the coast, where they changed back into their Western clothes. It is to be hoped the group had a flashlight and a compass for guidance, my father's account makes no mention of these attributes.

On March 2, on the beach, they spotted a sailing *prahu*; anchored offshore, they noticed two more serviceable ones they hoped would be available. But there were some difficulties. The vessels had been ordered by a resident of Timor to evacuate himself, his family, and a few Europeans, among them women and children. They could not in good conscience run off in the *prahus* without consent from the owner. Besides, they were warned that the crossover to one of the islands would be problematic, as there had been no wind to speak of for weeks, a situation my father and his friends were willing to risk.

Much to their regret, they lost precious time convincing the local authorities they needed the boats, as telephone communications had already been cut off. Finally, their request granted in view of their circumstances, they set sail in one of the *prahus* at sunset. They had used their waiting time to purchase food items from a small Chinese shop and some local roadside vendors. When they heard explosions to the east, they took it as a signal that their troops had blown up what was left of the military stores.

The party sailed north on hardly a breeze and arrived with a delay on March 4, at four o'clock in the afternoon at Alor, one of the many small islands east of Flores. While on the seas, they noticed a destroyer go by Wini, in all probability a Japanese one, at the same time that a bomber flew over their head without dropping a load, probably taking them for local fishermen.

Once on shore at Alor, they were received by a Dutch detachment that gave them permission to use one of its motor launches to reach Flores, provided they travel by night and spend the days on land.

The men motored along, passing one small island and then another, always at night, mooring in the early morning and making sure they were ahead of the Japs. Spotting a destroyer here and there in the distance, they reached the coast of Flores four days later, on March 8, relieved to finally hit land. A Catholic mission provided a truck that took them further on the road to Endeh, which they reached the next day, March 9.

Once in Endeh, they learned that the telegram they had sent from one of the islands to ask for further instructions had never arrived. Bali, the relay station, had fallen to the Japanese.

In Endeh, two more soldiers joined my father and his three friends, Lieutenant van den Dool, and Sergeant Kroese, sharing the same desire to escape and catch up with the Allied forces, somewhere, preferably on Java. Now they were a team of six.

On March 10, well stocked by the Catholic mission with cans of food and water, they continued by truck up-country to the town of Badjawa for deliberations. They contemplated acquiring a seaworthy *prahu* to sail across to Java. The conquest of Bali was a huge blow to their plans since the island was on the way to Java, their ultimate destination. Then, in the evening, on the radio, came another blow, this one worse. Java had surrendered. In the turn of a hand, the Japanese war machine had driven the British and Americans out of Singapore and the Philippines, yet they had always had their eye on the Netherlands Indies, and especially on Java, the large island rich in oil and minerals.

The town of Badjawa would forever remain in the recollection of the six men as the town where their respective destinies were forged.

Flores had not yet been occupied. My mother and her two children stayed with the Assistant Resident up-country in Badjawa. Without news, the future did not bode well.

My father caught up with us, but he knew we could not be together for long. Since the fall of Java, the six men were obliged to look at their situation from a different angle. They knew it would be unwise to stay on the island waiting for the Japanese, who were rapidly approaching. It was clear that they would be made prisoners of war, or since they were military, it was not inconceivable they would be executed. Australia was free and the Allied Army was there, so in their minds, sailing to Australia was the logical solution. My father and his group were still under military orders and their evacuation to Australia was a military operation, which meant that no families were allowed to come along. Besides, my father would have been reluctant to burden the group with a woman and two small children. At some point, the other men had already left their families behind.

For a few days, they looked around in Badjawa, but in the end, through intermediaries, they laid their hands on a sailing boat with an old hot bulb engine used by pearl fishers, a so-called pearling lugger. Her name was *Princess Mary*. She belonged to an Australian, Mr. Hilliard Sr., who owned a pearl fishing company in Perth, Australia. It was decided that three of the men would fetch the boat, which was moored on the west coast, and sail it to Aimere, the port town of Badjawa on the south coast. Lieutenant Stoll and the Sergeants de Maar and Meyer left on March 12 to pick her up. They first drove to the north harbor of Reo and then took a motor launch to the location of the vessel, where they arrived the next day late in the afternoon. The seven tonner *Princess Mary* measured about forty feet with three sails and a somewhat decrepit engine. It turned out that she needed a new mast, and with engine trouble on the way back, combined with a lack of a breeze, their arrival at Aimere was delayed until the early afternoon of March 19, when they immediately started to scrub the ship and make her ready. The other three had stayed in Badjawa to stock up on provisions, such as fuel, foodstuffs, blankets, and mats, for a journey that Mr. Hilliard estimated would take about two weeks. To be on the safe side, they made sure they had enough for a trip of one month.

On March 20, they loaded up a truck and made for Aimere.

The pearl schooner Princess Mary

Initially, the local crew, as well as the son of Mr. Hilliard, agreed to sail them across, as they were seasoned pearl fishers and well acquainted with the route. But suddenly, they recanted and flatly refused to come along. My father and his companions were faced with a big dilemma: They would have to make the crossing on their own, but could they do it? It was a daunting 700-mile expedition on a pearl schooner that, by the looks of it, was unstable and possibly rather leaky to boot. Besides, the northern coast of Australia was intimidating: it was barren, rocky, practically uninhabitable, and studded with numerous inlets and coves with thousands of treacherous small islands and reefs that could wreck an inexperienced sailor in no time at all. The huge difference of twelve to fourteen yards between high and low tide turned the water between the rocks and reefs into a menacing whirlpool. They also had to take under consideration the risk of getting caught by the Japanese navy and air force patrolling the waters in search of escapees.

As for experience: my father and Sergeant de Maar had done a lot of prize-winning sailing in their student days. Besides, de Maar had a notion about engines, and all of them owned a compass. On board, they found a map and a log. At any rate, they figured Australia, because it is such a large continent, could not be missed if they stuck to a south-southeast course. The men were optimistic and full of confidence in their capabilities. They decided to go ahead, their joint expertise would get them through. They may have been slightly naïve, ignorant of tides, cliffs, squalls, wind force, and all the other pitfalls on open seas under high skies, but their determination to reach safer land and the Allied forces overshadowed any critical thinking.

Then, for the second time, my parents had to say goodbye, infinitely more painful this time, Australia being so much further than Timor and the war clouds considerably heavier. How long would the separation last? What would happen in the coming years? Would a Japanese occupation be comparable to what they understood was happening in Europe at the onset of the war? Life seemed still relatively normal in the early weeks, barring the disgraceful persecution of the Jews. Or would it be worse in view of the disconcerting news that was trickling through from Java? Would they be alive when all was said and done?

My mother and her children stayed behind on the beach, forlorn, smaller and smaller, abandoned to fate, as the *Princess Mary* sailed off to Australia, disappeared on the horizon, and headed toward a fate of her own.

4

The *Princess Mary*

"The wind and the waves are always on the side of the ablest navigator."
~ Edward Gibbon (1737-1794)

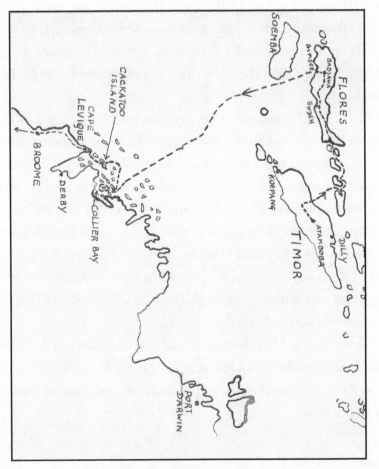

Map of Flores and crossing

On March 20, 1942, late in the afternoon, my father and his friends began their adventure. They sailed at dusk to avoid being spotted by the Japanese. In the beginning, all went well. The next day, they sighted the island of Sumba from a distance of six miles. But then the motor broke down, which from there on, it would do with maddening regularity. They set sail on a slight breeze until de Maar could restart the engine. It proved to become a habitual chore with the necessary participation of some or all of the crew. After a few hours, the engine gave up again, and as there was no wind, they just drifted along. Sumba was still in sight, although by now quite far behind. A light wind came up, which raised their spirits considerably. There was merriment and singing on board as they sailed on. These were the last happy hours for a couple of days.

On March 23, the wind grew into a vicious storm, forcing them to lower the fore and main topsails and forge ahead on just the jib sail. The waves crashed onto the decks in terrifying quantities and frequency. The tiny ship was tossed up and down, left and right; the crew became violently seasick, except Stoll and de Maar. A spare oil drum got loose from its ropes. It banged ferociously against the engine room and had to be rolled overboard, as it was impossible to refasten. The boom and the jib with the lowered sails swung dangerously close to their heads, the jib eventually smashing into the ocean, hitting the boat alongside with horrifying force. With great effort, they pulled it back in and secured it onto the mast.

Whether they were seasick or not, in turn, they had to pump the water out of the leaky craft every three hours, a grueling chore on a rolling vessel. Pumping needed to be done on a regular basis during their entire trip and was a task that tired them the most. If it was not the engine that needed to be pumped, it was the water pump or the primus stove for cooking. With each huge, fearsome wave they expected to go under. For two nights and two days the storm continued; cooking, eating, and sleeping were impossible, and so was resting or lying down for fear of being thrown overboard. Every now and then, they fed themselves on a can of milk. Their muscles were sore.

On March 26, to their relief, this northwestern storm abated, which gave them a chance to assess the damage. The fore-topsail could be re-hoisted, but the mainsail was totally destroyed and could not be repaired right away. When the wind died down completely, they were not so pleased anymore, as the motor had given up again. Instead of pumping water, they now had to pump air to start up the cylinders. It worked. The motor functioned for a few hours but then died once more. They floated along on a light south-southeast breeze, on heavy swells of an ever turbulent ocean. There was still no question of rest or food.

The crew: in the foreground left to right: Sgt. Meyer and Sgt. Kroese, in the background, Lt. Neeb, Sgt. De Maar, Lt. van den Dool, Lt. Stoll (The picture was taken with a self-timer)

March 27, a new day, began with repairs on the engine and its leaking cylinders. Again, they needed to pump air. They decided to use the motor at half capacity in order to spare the cylinders, as well as de Maar, who had been going nonstop, checking and repairing the engine.

On March 28, they put the motor to full use again, pushing along with a speed of three to four knots. At midday, there was more trouble. They sailed straight into a subtropical cyclone, coming from the south-west, accompanied by high winds and heavy rain showers that locals call a "cockeye," a frequent phenomenon along the north coast of Australia. They lowered the sails again, and for the second time found themselves in a storm, not knowing how long this one would last. Not too long, it turned out, and after one and a half hours of soaking rain and strong winds, they drifted on the waves, once more without the engine, so de Maar and the motor could rest.

At six o'clock in the morning on March 29, Stoll was the first to see land. He called out to the others, and all six of them stood on deck, waving, jumping, exhilarated. Their joy was short-lived, however, for it appeared to be an uninhabited island, one of the many that were part of a coral reef formation, which in the coming days would give them plenty of trouble. They continued, using the engine, steering a middle course through foam-crested waves, unaware that these waves were an indication of lurking danger.

They had arrived at Collier Bay, a dangerous area infested with coral reefs, and tried desperately to circumnavigate a few of the islands but instead grounded the vessel. They were able to pry it loose and chose to backtrack to the open sea, the darkening sky and the looks of the seething waves further down the bay scared them off. By then, it was six o'clock in the evening, they were relieved to be outside the bay, but within half an hour, they hit another reef.

As high tide approached, they lowered the anchor in hopes the rising water would lift them up again. Fifteen minutes later, another cockeye came their way with breathtaking speed from the east, the horizon pitch black with threatening cloud banks. Perhaps the whirlwinds pushed the waves because suddenly they were loose again, which enabled them to continue work on the ship, albeit in gushing rain and hurricane-force winds. They had just lowered the anchor, but then quickly pulled it back up. The engine was still warm and started immediately, and in haste, they sailed north, further into the open sea to get away as far as possible from the wretched reefs. For two hours, they battled the cockeye. The howling wind blew from starboard; the rain hurtled against their skin like hailstones; the small short waves sprayed the deck continuously.

Those of the sailors that were not needed on deck as helmsman or watch man took shelter in the engine room. The wind died down somewhat to a healthy breeze, and the man at the helm changed course toward the west, looking out for the foaming waves that betrayed dangerous reefs or islands. For the time being, all went well, though the crew was exhausted from the tension during the dim night in this particularly inclement stretch of the ocean. However, the men still needed all their navigation skills since over and over again they noticed many small islands and much foam. The schooner hardly made time, due to the strong tide against it.

March 30 was a day full of surprises. Suddenly, on starboard, they noticed small white spots on one of the islands and suspected they were huts or houses. They steered toward them and shared a few anxious moments crossing a reef bar before they could anchor in a narrow bay. It was a relief to be on land for once, on a stable surface. The houses were abandoned and empty, barring one or two pieces of rickety furniture. In one of the rooms that must have served as an office, they found a budget sheet printed with "Australian Steel and Iron Corporation Yampi Operations." They had stumbled upon a mine. On another dusty table they came across a list of arrivals and departures of ships to Derby, which made them conclude they were possibly somewhere in the neighborhood of this town.

The men decided to split into two groups to explore the island further, two of them returning to the ship. In the mine itself, they found nothing, but in one of the buildings, they happily located a can of oil, which they very much needed, as their fuel was getting dangerously low. But sadly, the oil proved too dirty to be of any use. They looked forward to staying on the island, paradise in their view, for a day to rest and to do some necessary repairs on ropes, sails, and of course, on the engine. They replenished their drinking water supply from the many rainwater barrels.

While the four of them were having a great time, they suddenly heard excited shouts from the direction of the ship; the two men who had returned were in a panic. They ran to the beach and saw their *Princess Mary* slowly but surely slant to starboard. The ebb had grounded her. The difference between ebb and flood must have been nearly eight yards, they guessed. Nothing more happened to the ship; she stayed slanted until high water when the crew took her out of the bay and moored her onto a buoy.

On March 31, midday, a small sailing boat came their direction from the north. They quickly completed the inevitable repairs, fervently hoping that this little vessel could pilot them through the maze of cliffs, reefs, and islands. As the boat approached, they detected her name: *Blanche*. They called out to the sailors of the lugger if they could follow them to another town, hopefully Broome. Two Australians, Chris and Ginger Hunter, were on board with three aborigines. They agreed, and after hurriedly hoisting the sails, the *Princess Mary* followed the *Blanche*.

That evening, they anchored near an island; it was too dangerous to sail at night. The crew of the *Blanche*, fishermen from Cape Levique, the lighthouse, knew the area well. They informed my father and his friends that they had encountered their problems near Cacatoo Island on the east coast of Kings Sound, Derby's Bay, notorious for its dangerous cliffs, reefs, tides, and rip currents. They should count their blessings they were not shipwrecked; it would have been the perfect spot for such a disaster.

On April 1, the two ships left on a tide between the reefs that had transformed itself into a monstrous, whirling river. They were dragged along, now totally out of control; sometimes they sailed backward, sometimes diagonally, sometimes a mere few yards from looming rocks. It proved impossible for the *Princess Mary* to follow the pilot any longer.

At times, the schooner was miles ahead. At other times, the *Blanche* was way out. Occasionally, both ships lost sight of each other for a full hour. Deep into Kings Sound, my father and his crew heard the roar of the waves against the reefs and knew they were still in the danger zone, fearing their ship would crash any moment.

By mid-afternoon, the *Blanche* had sailed so far ahead that they continued on the engine to catch up with her and requested that they be tugged for a stretch. Chris Hunter transferred to the *Princess Mary* and adroitly sailed the two connected ships around menacing reefs and cliffs to the west shore of Kings Sound. They arrived in the early evening.

On April 2, at eleven forty-five in the morning, the tide in their favor, the *Princess Mary* sailed with great speed along the coast between reef thresholds and small rocks toward what could possibly be their final destination.

They were gripped with a deep sense of relief. It seemed that the end of their ordeal was near. Chris Hunter had left the *Blanche* at Kings Sound in the care of the aboriginal crew and steered the *Princess Mary* through the waters that he knew so well, straight toward Cape Levique. In the early evening, they anchored near the lighthouse. Sergeant Meyer and Sergeant Kroese stepped ashore to meet with the two lighthouse keepers, Wood and Goldring.

They were on land, the ocean and its dangers behind them.

They sent the following telegram to the Netherlands Consulate in Sydney:

"Three Dutch officers and three Dutch N.C.O. arrived at Cape Levique, escaped from Timor, asking instructions."

The owners of the *Princess Mary* in Perth received another telegram:

"Your Princess Mary lais (sic) at Cape Levique. Hilliard sent her."

The lighthouse keepers suggested the men use a truck to drive to Broome. Their luggage was taken off the *Princess Mary*. They charged Chris Hunter, their trustworthy and seasoned pilot, with sailing the ship to a safe place. Wood and Goldring kept the remnants of the provisions and invited them to spend the night at the lighthouse, in peace and quiet.

April 3, 1942, was a momentous day. They stood on firm ground. They had made it, six former strangers whose mutual support had enabled them to survive the desperate voyage. From one of the dunes, they gazed over the ocean that could well have been their grave, a dark sky to the east heralding the arrival of another cockeye, which they could now watch in safety, in awe of its power and ominous beauty. They reminisced about their adventure and exchanged thoughts and worries, for which they now had time. On board, they had been too busy or too sick.

It had taken them from March 20 to April 3 to cross from Flores to the coast of Australia, in a barely serviceable pearl schooner, with a limited pool of know-how, across 700 miles over unfamiliar waters. Yet, they met the challenge, well equipped with physical strength and determination.

On April 4, a small truck arrived from Broome to pick them up for the trip southward. This time, their hazards appeared on land in the form of muddy and sandy terrain. More than once, the men had to dig out the truck from deep ruts, pushing and pulling to move it a yard or two. After eight hours, they were forty-seven miles south of Cape Levique, spending the night at a place called Beagle Bay Mission, and the next day, traveled the last ninety-nine miles to Broome.

From April 6 to April 9, they stayed in Broome, resting while waiting for further transportation to the south. Three weeks earlier, Broome had been the scene of multiple Japanese air attacks on Dutch and American Catalina's and other flying boats, carrying refugees from the Dutch East Indies. At low tide, my father and his crew surveyed the pieces of wreckage, searching for names and valuables. The decaying suitcases still contained shreds of clothing, the burnt-out planes were covered with acorn shells, and handbags, hats, shoes, and toys were visible under a thin layer of silt. It was a grim scene.

Part of the luggage and toys belonged to the widow and young son of the late Rear Admiral Karel Doorman, Commander of the Combined Striking Force, the Allied fleet that attempted to obstruct, or at least slow down, the Japanese invasion during the battle of the Java Sea. She and her son managed to escape in a Catalina from Java after her husband's cruiser went down. Some of the child's toys are now in the Broome Museum. Both mother and son survived the attack, though wounded and burned, and forever plagued with harrowing memories of fuel on fire around them while swimming for more than an hour in the ocean before being rescued. The son, Theo, happens to be a friend of my brother Peter.

A few days later, my father and his companions learned that on that same day of the attack on the Catalina's, a Japanese Zero had also shot down a Dutch airplane that was en route from Java to Broome, a DC-3 named *Pelikaan*. Before taking off from Bandung, Captain Ivan Smirnoff, a naturalized Dutchman of Russian origin, received a package, a cigar box in brown paper, with instructions to hand it over to the Commonwealth Bank in Broome. Captain Smirnoff managed to nosedive the plane into the water after it was shot, but with this maneuver, the package slipped out of the first-aid compartment where Smirnoff had stored it. It turned out that the missing cigar box contained diamonds with a value of $20 million today, although Smirnoff did not know it. The crew survived, but the whereabouts of the diamonds remain a mystery until this day. Several authors have written books about this episode, the crew has been suspected, and beachcombers have been on trial, and speculations still abound.

On April 10, at five-thirty in the morning, the six men took a plane from Broome south to Perth, arriving at three o'clock in the afternoon. It is surprising how long this flight took; either the plane was slow or it speaks of the enormous distances across Australia.

In Perth, they were received by a group of journalists who had heard about their trek through Timor and the journey on the *Princess Mary*.

The following article appeared in the *Sunday Times* on April 12, 1942:

Sunday Times (Perth, WA), Sunday, 12 April 1942

Nightmare Voyage from Timor

DUTCH DOCTOR'S THRILLING ESCAPE

As thrilling as fiction is the story of the escape from Timor of four Dutch officers who recently arrived at an Australian city.
Disguised as natives in a desperate trek through miles of jungle and finding themselves in a small sailing boat with only themselves to navigate, the men reached a point on the

north-west coast of Australia after a fortnight at sea during which they survived three storms.

The story was told yesterday by tall, blond Dr. H. Neeb, a medical officer with the rank of lieutenant in the Netherlands East Indies Army.

"We were at Koepang at the time the Japanese launched their attack at one-thirty a.m. on February 20," he stated.

"The Japs came by sea and landed 20,000 troops and mechanized units, including armored cars, tanks, and motorcycles.

"At the break of dawn 800 para-troops were dropped, followed up by 500 more next day.

"Our defenses could not stand up to the overwhelming odds. We were forced to retreat, and our forces became split up.

"The troops were ordered to retreat to a town called Atamboea, which is 200 miles from Koepang and in the center of Timor.

"It took us four days to reach Atamboea, here we found other Dutch and Australian troops.

"The O.C. of Atamboea then gave the order that it was every party for themselves.

We, in our party, knew of two harbors on the north of the island, one sixty miles away, and the other twenty miles away.

THROUGH THE JUNGLE

"We set out for the former by motor car. At the end of thirty miles, we abandoned the car and went a further thirty miles on foot through the jungle.

"Meanwhile we could hear the Japs bombing the other harbor and were thankful that we had selected the furthest one. From here we disguised ourselves as best we could, as natives.

"Arriving at the coast we got hold of a fishing boat, thirty feet in length, and set out for the island of Alor.

"During the trip Jap planes flew over us, imagining us to be fishermen. A Jap destroyer nosed into view under ten miles away, but again, the enemy disdained to investigate us.

"After arriving at Alor we called at numerous islands, replenishing our supplies of water, and we finally reached Flores.

"Just off Flores we sighted a Japanese fleet, and, hastily picking up two other Dutch officers, we took to a pearling lugger, the crew of which undertook to navigate us across to Darwin.

"We had first intended sailing westward from this point to Java but changed our plans when we heard of the Jap landings on the island.

TRYING JOURNEY

"At the last minute, the crew refused to sail with us. We were desperate and took off by ourselves with only a compass and common sense to guide us.

"It took us a fortnight—a nightmare trip—to reach Australia. Three storms threatened to sink us. We were blown off our course each time. Food and water gave out, and we were not unhappy to strike the Australian coast at Collier Bay.

"Hugging the coast, we then proceeded southwards. Reefs made this voyage a hazardous one.

"Finally we reached Cockatoo Island and met two fishermen there who said they would guide us to Cape Levique. We were very grateful to them.

"From Cape Levique word of our plight was sent to Broome and we were duly picked up and brought to that port."

Lieutenant Neeb added that he and his fellow officers are anxious to rejoin the Dutch army again and to fight alongside the Australians, whom, he said, had met them with kindness everywhere."

Here the newspaper column ends.

Nightmare Voyage From Timor

Dutch Doctor's Thrilling Escape

As thrilling as fiction is the story of the escape from Timor of four Dutch officers who recently arrived at an Australian city.

Disguised as natives in a desperate trek through miles of jungle and finding themselves in a small sailing boat with only themselves to navigate, the men reached a point on the north-west coast of Australia after a fortnight at sea, during which they survived three storms.

The story was told yesterday by tall, blonde Dr. H. Neeb, medical officer with the rank of lieutenant in the Netherlands East Indies Army.

"We were at Koepang at the time the Japanese launched their attack at 1.0 a.m. on February 20," he stated.

"The Japs came by sea and landed 20,000 troops and mechanised units, including armored cars, tanks and motor cycles.

"At the break of dawn 800 paratroops were dropped, followed up by 500 more next day.

"Our defences could not stand up to the overwhelming odds. We were forced to retreat, and our forces became split up.

"The troops were ordered to retreat to a town called Atam-

DR. H. NEEB, lieutenant in the N.E.I. Army, who has reached Australia after an adventurous trip (see story this page).

boea," which is 200 miles from Koepang and in the centre of Timor.

"It took us four days to reach Atamboea, where we found other Dutch and Australian troops.

"The O.C. of Atamboea then gave the order that it was every party for themselves.

"We, in our party, knew of two harbors on the north of the island, one 60 miles away and the other 20 miles.

Through Jungle

"We set out for the former by motor car. At the end of 30 miles we abandoned the car and went a further 30 miles on foot through the jungle.

"Meanwhile we could hear the Japs bombing the other harbor

and were thankful that we had selected the furthest one. From here we disguised ourselves, as best we could, as natives.

"Arriving at the coast we got hold of a fishing boat, 30 feet in length, and set out for the island of Alor.

"During the trip Jap planes flew over us, but took no notice of us, imagining us to be fishermen. A Jap destroyer nosed into view under 10 miles away, but again the enemy disdained to investigate us.

"After arriving at Alor we called at numerous islands, replenishing our supplies of water, and we finally reached Flores.

"Just off Flores we sighted a Japanese fleet, and, hastily picking up two other Dutch officers, we took to a pearling lugger, the crew of which undertook to navigate us across to Darwin.

"We had first intended sailing westward from this point to Java, but changed our plans when we heard of the Jap landings on the island.

Trying Journey

"At the last minute the crew refused to sail with us. We were desperate and took off by ourselves with only a compass and commonsense to guide us.

"It took us a fortnight—a nightmare trip—to reach Australia. Three storms threatened to sink us. We were blown off our course each time. Food and water gave out, and we were not unhappy to strike the Australian coast at Collier Bay.

"Hugging the coast, we then proceeded southwards. Reefs made this voyage a hazardous one.

"Finally we reached Cockatoo Island and met two fishermen there who said they would guide us to Cape Levique. We were very thankful to them.

"From Cape Levique word of our plight was sent to Broome and we were duly picked up and

Lieutenant Neeb added that he and his fellow officers are anxious to rejoin the Dutch army again and to fight alongside the Australians, whom, he said, had met them with kindness everywhere.

The article erroneously listed that the escape was accomplished by four Dutch officers. In actuality, the crew consisted of six men, three of them were officers and the other three N.C.O.'s.

My father and his companions stayed in Perth until April 23. A ship took them to their final destination, Melbourne, where they arrived a week later, on April 30, 1942.

The journey was accomplished.

Post Script:

For Lieutenant Stoll, his escape from Timor was to be his last journey. On December 1, 1942, he and his unit of sixty-two men was on its way to Timor to replace a Dutch detachment when the Australian Corvette that carried them was destroyed in an enemy air raid. All on board were killed.

Lieutenant van den Dool died of a heart attack in Hollandia, New Guinea, in 1945.

Sergeant Meyer was shot down in 1944.

Sergeant de Maar joined the Allied Army and, after the war, chose to remain in Australia.

Sergeant Kroese joined the Allied Army and returned to the Netherlands in 1945.

Lieutenant Neeb, my father, joined the Allied Army. He traveled around the continent of Australia on various assignments, as well as all over the Pacific Ocean. During this time, he repeatedly tried to find out what had happened to his family, but his continuous search yielded no clues until the end of the war.

From the town of Merauke on the south coast of New Guinea, which had not been taken by the Japanese, he worked from 1942 until 1944 to alleviate malaria and other tropical diseases. In 1945, he was affiliated with the Australian and American forces in the

Pacific when they re-conquered the oil refineries both in Northern Borneo (the island of Tarakan) and on Morotai in the Molucca islands. He tended the sick and wounded, among whom were many battle casualties. Melbourne called him back regularly for reports.

As extensive as my father's records are about the events at the beginning of the war, he ceased making notes upon his arrival in Melbourne in April 1942. The paragraph above is a summary of the itineraries he had jotted down on slips of paper that were simply clipped onto his prior accounts. All in all, his war years since he landed in Melbourne come across as a fascinating span, notwithstanding the obvious suspense and anxieties, but he was, at minimum, spared the horrors of a Japanese prisoner of war camp, and probable death.

After a period of a few years in Dutch New Guinea in the towns of Hollandia and Ifar, my father finally settled in the Netherlands.

5

Captivity — From Riches
to Rags

"No arts; no letters; no society; and which is worst of all,
continual fear and danger of violent death; and the life of man,
solitary, poor, nasty, brutish and short."
~ Thomas Hobbes (1588-1679)

The house in Endeh was bare except for a few borrowed pieces
of furniture for my mother and her toddlers. My father's ship
had disappeared over the horizon. Peter suffered from dysentery,
while I was ailing with kidney trouble. The only remaining doctor
on the island was a Chinese man who had just let a child die through
incompetence. My mother's friends up-country offered lodgings
again, but she preferred to stay in Endeh, anxious to learn what
would happen next. With the fall of Java, the Japanese could hit
Flores any time. The local population, totally perplexed and unable
to continue its daily routine, went around in a daze, especially when
the able men were summoned to dig shelters that, in spite of all their
efforts, turned out to be no more than holes in the ground.

Then, in May 1942, the Japanese invasion of Flores finally
happened.

They began their occupation by ordering full-scale house arrests.
It was how my mother celebrated her twenty-sixth birthday on May

20, with her two children and the *babu*. The Japanese strictly forbade people to leave home, other than at a regular pre-approved time for food shopping or a doctor's appointment. They allowed families to keep one servant. Any transgression would be punished, and soon enough, it became clear what the punishment entailed. The Japs were everywhere, carloads of them, like ants. Upon their arrival, they massacred local people whom they suspected of having loyalties to the Europeans—no more cozy relations with despicable imperialists. The Chinese citizens were especially targeted since Japan continued to consider itself at war with China.

The soldiers enjoyed themselves, doing gymnastics on open fields to stay fit. They followed the Europeans and the locals around, making sure it was understood who was the boss. It was obvious they had a good time. They were the conquerors; we were the weak ones who had let ourselves be overpowered. The Japs swaggered about, bellowed orders, menacingly hit their boots with their batons. They were noisy and, needless to say, very unfriendly. The population felt intimidated, which was the sole intention. People looked over their shoulder to check if they were safe and hurried home; the shopping tours were unpleasant.

But, at the local market, the only place for her social contacts, my mother briefly met with some of her friends. Occasionally she went by the hospital to get medication for the family, which gave her a chance to visit with the nuns; Peter and I had recovered, but my mother liked a well-stocked medicine cabinet. The children usually stayed at home with the *babu*.

On one of those scary shopping outings, she sensed she was being followed. It was a very hot day in the middle of the dry monsoon. She did not know whether to run or to pretend she did not notice her pursuer. The heat was oppressive, and she panted with fear. But there was no more time to think. Before she knew what to do, the

Jap grabbed her, threw her to the ground, and raped her. Her shopping trip turned into the day she would be raped. This was a scar she would have to carry with her throughout her imprisonment, hardly a time propitious for soul-searching, when she would need all her resources for the survival of herself and her two children. There were no social workers; she did not have the help of grief counselors. By her own strength, she would have to try and heal before her detention, during her time in the camps, and forever afterward.

The soldier fled and my mother made it home. In typical Japanese fashion, anger, madness, hysterics were followed by kindness and remorse, which my mother was to taste in good measure in the future. The rapist came to our bungalow and gave her money, which my mother passed on to the nuns for their charity work. Her comfort was the affection of the Sisters Berneria and Renalda.

The house arrests lasted until July 1942.

Open trucks rolled into Endeh, so called three-tonners, with soldiers in the back wildly brandishing their loaded guns in a show of strength, a futile demonstration as there were just women, children, and some clergy in town to be shipped off, but scary nonetheless. The Europeans were ordered to gather in the center square, the ones who lived up-country had been transported down in the meantime with a few of their personal belongings. The next order was to go home, pack only one suitcase, and return to the square within an hour. My mother disobeyed, grabbed two suitcases instead, some medicines, and even a small mattress. The *babu* helped her pack and accompanied her with the luggage and the children back to town. At the square followed a tearful farewell from a loyal servant who had been with the family since 1938, barely three years ago. They held hands for a long time, and both my mother and the *babu* cried. It was all so bitter, so unjust, and so frightening.

In order to facilitate whatever plans they had in mind, the Japs loaded the crowd onto the trucks, aiming their guns at the group that had swelled into, by my mother's calculations, close to 200 people, including the clergy. After a short ride to a nearby inn, the soldiers unloaded their captives and demanded they stay together inside, even prohibiting them from stepping out onto the verandah.

There was hardly any room; there were not enough chairs or sofas, not enough beds. Space was tight. The Japanese policy was to amass as many people as humanly possible into small places, in order to economize on guards. The army needed their men to fight, not to monitor prisoners. The group stayed at the crowded inn for a few days, all this time kept in the dark as to a next move. The place was uncomfortable, the women were nervous and irritable, the children kept whining, sleep was a problem, and food was another problem. The Japs provided the meals, rice, and a vegetable, but they developed a habit of skipping a dinner or two. The nuns did what they could to be helpful, Sisters Berneria and Renalda still looking out for my mother and her two toddlers. But where had the priests gone?

The occupation of the Pacific Rim by the Japanese was an extremely well-oiled machine. Once the conquest was complete, the scene became one of feverish activity. They wasted no time. Ships ferried back and forth between the islands to fetch men, women, and children to drop them off at the numerous camps that had been quickly established all over their newly acquired territories. In order to spread the soldiers rapidly out over the landscape, they even used bicycles. Thousands of trucks went by cities and villages up-country, sparing no island, no nation; the people became full-fledged prisoners the moment they went through the gates. The Japs built new camps with bamboo and straw; other detention centers were refurbished residential quarters, schools, institutions, or temples even. They meted out a different fate to the military, the Prisoners of War, or POWs, who were forced into camps of their own.

The Pacific Rim was the theater of approximately 360 civilian camps in total, 300 of them in the Dutch East Indies. 123,000 Caucasian civilians were interned. 6,200 Americans, 900 Americans in the Dutch East Indies alone. The 140,000 POWs, thousands of Americans among the Allies, were held in their own 100 camps specifically for the military, which made it a total of approximately 460 camps, give or take a few. Japanese command and the camp heads never accurately recorded the figures. Outside the Dutch East Indies, there were camps for civilians and POWs in Japan, China, Thailand, Hong Kong, the Philippines, Burma, Singapore, and on the Pacific Islands. Over a period of nearly four years, the Pacific Rim was practically one large concentration camp. The prisoners began to understand what the Greater East Asia Co-Prosperity Sphere was all about.

On July 19, 1942, one of those busy ferry ships arrived to pick us up from the inn near Endeh and drop us off who knows where. We packed suitcases and belongings again, and this time the group was driven to the jetty instead of inland.

In the hot sun in the open truck, my mother with her children and the others waited for several hours until we were told to board. These ships were not very large, and as this particular one had picked up the Europeans from various islands, and included the group of 200 from Endeh, it was, of course, overcrowded. My mother found out that our destination was Macassar on the south coast of Celébes, the city that my grandparents had enjoyed barely seven months ago, in another time, in another world.

It was at that point that my mother lost sight of her beloved nuns, Berneria and Renalda. The other nuns were there, but not her two dear ones. As she went around the crowded vessel to secure a place for the three of us, she kept looking for the sisters and asked about them, but to no avail, which has always remained a mystery to her. The spot we had been allotted was untenable. We sat on the sloping lid of a cargo hold, close to a drain with filthy water. Peter slipped down continuously with the drain at his feet. I did my very best to hold him back. My mother returned without much hope; the only place she had found was one just slightly off the drain.

The days were long; the nights were even longer. It took four days to cross to Macassar. After the first uncomfortable night, my mother, leaning against some tightly roped cargo with her toddlers in her lap, wanted to explore the ship a little further. She asked a friendly woman to watch her two suitcases and the mattress, precious items, while she took the children and started walking the decks.

Her thinking was that since the ship had been rolling and bumping through the night, whatever was on the ship, people and cargo, might have rolled with it as well like marbles in a tin and become displaced. She was right, and to her joy, she located a bench, only half occupied, that could accommodate one of her children. She stowed the mattress underneath to hold another child, and she herself would rest against the side of the bench. At least the three of us were now far removed from the dirty drain.

In spite of this new arrangement, we did not sleep well, nor were we fed adequately, as the passengers were told to cook their own meals, which was no sinecure with wood that was wet. Torpedoes were all around; the danger of being blown up was not imaginary. We were told not to wave at anything we spotted, lest we should be discovered, which my mother thought was quite silly, as the ship was certainly larger than a few waving hands.

But by then, we knew better than to argue with our masters. Looking around her oppressive environment of dirt and chaos, it was unavoidable that my mother's thoughts went back to the order and comfort of the Vliethuis. Her next thoughts were: "How did I get here, and why?" These were more questions of bewilderment than ones she expected to be answered. From modern civilization, she found herself reduced to a stone-age existence, perhaps even worse than Stone Age because of the hostile control of her captors.

During the four days and nights of the crossing, the women managed to establish a routine, relationships were forged, and commiseration helped to carry them along, as the fate of each and every person appeared to be identical. They suspected they were all going to the same place, wherever that place would be. They learned to help each other, to be generous with advice and, when necessary, to share food. These four days proved to be proper training for the future.

The ship moored at the pier of Macassar. They gathered their belongings again. My mother was given a helping hand down the gangway with her two suitcases, her mattress, and her two toddlers. Then followed another spell of waiting in the hot sun for the next orders. They sat on their luggage, thirsty and tired. Finally, several trucks showed up to take them to the military barracks. Odd as it may seem, these lodgings came as a relief, for after several days, they were finally able to change clothes and refresh themselves, never mind that the women were warned not to waste any water and were told to bathe together, all of them with their children, at the same time.

These barracks were going to be chock-full as well. The first group to arrive was the group of 200 from Endeh, along with the passengers of the other islands on the same ship; then more Europeans arrived from the island of Celebes, where Macassar itself was located. My mother realized she quickly had to mark her territory and found a corner, where she put down her mattress and the children. The routine was the same, sleep and no sleep, food and no food, noise, and whining children, my mother's children included. Hygiene was manageable, an improvement on what they had to endure on the ship. Again, there was uncertainty. "What was behind all this? Were these rumors about prison camps true? How long would they be held captive? Would conditions improve?" There were no answers; they were at the mercy of their captors.

After one month at the military barracks, another order was issued to move the prisoners by a truck caravan into the mountains, to Malino, located about forty-five miles east of Macassar. Because the ferry ships were unable to handle any more passengers, the remaining captives were transported inland. These truck rides, under the tropical sun, were fearsome. As a rule, there was no tailgate; drivers were whipping around bends and slamming on the brakes. The passengers were tossed about and had to hang onto each other and their luggage in order to stay inside the truck bed. My mother preferred to sit on her suitcases, holding tightly to her children; her view was reduced to the legs, socks, and shoes around her.

It was August 1942. My mother had watched the *Princess Mary* vanish over the horizon in March, nearly five months ago. She did not know if her husband made it to Australia, and she would not know until the war had come to an end.

Malino offered another type of imprisonment. It was a resort town, cool, high in the mountains, with attractive vacation homes and company bungalows. These were confiscated by the Japanese. The ones located close together were marked for our confinement. Truckloads full of prisoners had arrived before the evacuation of my mother's group from Macassar, and the houses were already filled to capacity. Once the Macassar trucks were unloaded, people had to hang around again, this time for nearly three hours, until the Japs figured out where to deposit all these new arrivals.

They piled the group of our transport into several of the already overcrowded houses, with the result that each home ended up containing about forty women and children, the children would have to sleep in the kitchen cabinets. A housing committee was installed to oversee the proper running of the entire encampment and to make sure instructions were duly carried out. Since her departure from Endeh in May, my mother still was not used to sharing a small space with a lot of bodies, this time with forty women and many children, but the past three months had taught her she had no option except to adjust. This was not always the case with the new arrivals. Personalities clashed, and at times, conflicts proved impossible to resolve. The housing committee had to be called in to arrange for a separation or a move to a different home.

There was no ban yet on leaving the compound for the market, although the hours were restricted. The Japanese commandant had dismissed the servants some time ago, and whatever the women bought, they needed to lug back to the compound themselves.

Japanese guards

It did not help that books, magazines, newspapers, and radios were taken away and burned. There were regular house searches by the guards who warned that if anything was found amiss, severe beatings would follow. The time was filled with caring for the children and with multiple chores. My mother tried to establish a routine in the house she was assigned to. In agreement with a few other women, she created a kitchen detail, a cleaning shift, and a shopping team to check out the local market. They were making the best of their setting.

But very soon, the commandant decided to squeeze the few comforts they had available, and next came the order to hand over all their money. In one moment, the trips to the market were a thing of the past. Before my mother handed over her cash, she went out quickly to try and purchase some toiletries and a few bananas, yet, before long Japanese officers showed up, and that was the end of shopping. Local vendors were not allowed to sell to the women; transgression by the seller or the buyer would incur punishment. But what was there to buy without cash?

Three women were charged with the distribution of foodstuffs, which took place in one of the barracks at the market. My mother's shopping team would go and collect the provisions. Cooking was done on little wood stoves; the wood had to be hauled also.

It is ironic that by having been obliged to hand over their money to the Japanese commandant, the prisoners were, in reality, financing their very own captivity. The months went by, the routine became more acceptable, the chores easier, yet emotionally what was happening was almost unbearable. On top of losing their freedom and having to live in squalor, the married women did not know where and how their husbands were.

What they had picked up from the market gossip were stories of cruelty and torture in the men's and boys' camps, murders and executions even. It was useless to speculate what kind of atrocities were committed and whether their husbands and sons had succumbed. My mother, of course, knew that my father had sailed to Australia, but had he made it safely?

In December, the wet monsoon set in, and all day long, day in, day out, the rain continued. Typical of this season, it brought cloud bursts that turned into deluges. Diapers and clothing on ropes inside had to be ducked constantly and would not dry, but the wet clothes improved the acoustics. The air was hot and humid. The humidity caused an itchy rash that would not heal. Scratching only produced bloody sores that got infected. There was no medicine. The only hope was the advent of the dry monsoon, starting somewhere between March and May.

After approximately eight months in the Malino camp, May brought activity from the Japanese commando post in Macassar. Representatives were meeting off and on with the housing committee, and it was rumored that another displacement was imminent. My mother had been jostled around many times by now, from her home in Endeh by truck to the inn, by truck unto a ship for four days, then off the ship on a truck to the barracks in Macassar, from these barracks on a truck to Malino, each time with two toddlers, two suitcases, and a mattress. She was loath to have to set out on another expedition, and even more so this time, as she was told she could not take her mattress and only one of her two suitcases. Bad as Malino was, she had become used to the place, and the Japanese guards, although unsavory, were not the lunatics she had heard about. She put as many outfits as possible on her children, dressed herself in one frock over another with as much lingerie as she could handle and, with a heavy heart, waited for the events to unfold.

The trucks geared up, twenty to twenty-five of them. Where would they take more than 1,000 women and children? It was to the camp of Kampili, about thirty miles south from Macassar. With Malino located in the mountains, it promised to be a long trip and very hot at sea level. The soldiers divided the prisoners into three groups, each of a little more than 400 people, split up again into smaller sizes. Over three days, one group a day, the twenty or more trucks would transport the captives to their destination. A fixed bayonet was a warning not to grumble and obey.

My mother, Peter, and I were in the last group. The ride was as to be expected, four hours long, bumpy, and hot in an overcrowded truck with screeching stops and starts, and scary corners. My mother was glad to be finally unloaded at Kampili and to be able to stretch her legs.

Kampili, in better days, functioned as a tuberculosis sanitarium with a few small cement houses. It was a two-acre enclosure located near a canal between two major airfields. Our lodgings, surrounded by barbed wire, were twelve large barracks that had been under construction while the women and children were in Malino. The walls consisted of woven bamboo mats, home to bugs and insects. The hip roofs were covered with grass, the floors plain dirt, red dirt in this part of the world. A slit between the walls and the roof allowed for some light and draft. Each barrack held a hundred people, accommodating fifty beds on each side, double-deckers, two bunks above each other. The width did not exceed twenty inches per bunk. There was nothing in the way of furnishings, nor was there water or electricity. It was August, the red dust and dirt were everywhere.

Kampili was to be the camp of approximately 1,640 women and children.

When we arrived, we waited around again in the hot sun until we were allocated a barrack and a bunk. The cement houses were occupied by a large group of women and children that had arrived six weeks prior from the island of Ambon. These prisoners were bombed out when the Allies blew up a Japanese munition depot, hitting their camp in the process, which was at that time a family camp. Children were left orphans, women lost children, people lost limbs, all their possessions were gone in the fire. Before the bombardment, a dysentery epidemic had claimed many lives as well. The men were taken away to the men's camps. Some of my mother's group shared a brew of coffee and their grim stories with the Ambon women, until we could be herded to our respective barracks.

The three of us were assigned barrack number six; we were given only two racks as Peter and I, toddlers, were to share one, which we learned to do with my feet toward Peter's head and vice-versa. My mother took the upper rack; Peter and I stayed close to the ground and the dirt.

Interior of a camp barrack with children

The camp was divided into three blocks, two of six barracks, the third block consisted of the cement houses with the women and children from Ambon. The nuns stayed in the first barrack of our block, ninety-two of them. Barrack number eight of the second block housed the non-Dutch group, with a surprising assortment of nationalities. These included three American missionaries, an orthodox Jewish family, an Armenian family, some people of Scottish and Irish descent, and Russians as well. Besides English spoken, the lingua franca was Malay.

Each block had a blockhead as a liaison with the commandant; conversation with him was also in Malay. Being the blockhead was a demanding job, undesirable for sure, and only a woman with an obvious strong character would be selected. Any contact with our Japanese lord and master required tactfulness, patience, perseverance. The grievances, the lack of food and medicine, the work quotas, the health crises needed to be brought to his attention, yet always risked incurring wrath and beatings.

Our commandant was Yamaji Tadashi. He was short like most Japanese people, fat, had bowlegs, his hairstyle was a spiky crew cut, his teeth were tobacco stained. He wore dark-rimmed glasses and oversized boots. Although Kampili was totally isolated, there was absolutely no communication in any way, shape or form with the outside world, once or twice a rumor did make it through, and the one about Yamaji was enough to fill the women with dread. He was said to have a maniacal temper when he was the commander of the men's camp Pare Pare about a hundred miles from Kampili and had beaten an inmate to death. His punishment of choice in true Bushido fashion was beating with a tree branch until either he or the victim collapsed: Yamaji of exhaustion, the victim of wounds and bruises. The men of Pare Pare, who had wives and children in Kampili, were aghast that this brute was appointed their commandant.

As soon as Yamaji arrived in Kampili, he taught the women the basic rules for *tenko* or roll call, to be applied every time the prisoners crossed the shadow of a Japanese individual, be it of a visitor, an inspector, or of Yamaji himself. In the mornings, at seven o'clock or before, Yamaji went around the barracks to count noses, and expected *tenko*. It was the bowing ceremony, not intended as a sign of respect to him personally, but meant to honor the emperor in the person of the commandant. Failing to bow, which amounted to failing to show respect, would be asking for a beating. Soon Peter and I picked up the terms of *"kiotseke," "keirei,"* and *"naore,"* which we pronounced as "jotke," "kere," and "nore" ("attention," "bow," and "at ease"). My mother abhorred these demonstrations of humility, but to the children, the military precision of the roll calls was exciting.

The camp doctor, Dr. Marseille; a protestant minister, Spreeuwenberg; and a priest, Fr. Beltjens, served in the camp under the disguise of carpenters, handymen, and butchers, trades they had to learn on the spot. Men were not allowed in the camp, Yamaji was adamant, "They only make babies," but he knuckled under when he saw the advantages of a few handy fellows around. Besides the commandant and his aide, these three were the only men. They were allocated one of the cement houses.

For Dr. Marseille, there would not be much employment, as there was no medicine available. All he could do was diagnose issues, have the patient moved to the makeshift hospital, speak soothing words, and try to intervene with Yamaji for supplies from Macassar to no avail. He was successful only once when the number of rabid dogs around the camp got out of hand. A child had already died from a bite; a woman who fought a dog was on her deathbed; at night, the dogs howled and roamed around the latrines. Dr. Marseille managed to persuade Yamaji to order serum from the Pasteur Institute in Bandung, which did help one or two victims, but for others, it came too late.

Every now and then, the Protestant minister, Spreeuwenberg, was allowed to hold a Sunday evening prayer in the so-called church barrack. For the priest, Fr. Beltjens, a confessional stall was improvised in a corner of one of the storage houses of the Ambon women, using the only existing ramshackle chair and table on the grounds. In addition, both the minister and the priest as well as Dr. Marseille, applied their newly acquired trades.

Pastor Spreeuwenberg was an example of the strength of the human spirit and faith. Before the war, he lost a child to dysentery. When imprisoned at Ambon with his wife and two remaining children, he lost another child to typhoid fever and, in the bombardment, he lost his last child, while his wife, now interned with him at Kampili, got severely injured and lost her mind.

Father Beltjens, a man of a good-natured disposition, performed his priestly duties very early in the morning and would leave later for the slaughterhouse with a few boys to butcher pigs at the piggery for the Japanese kitchens in Macassar and elsewhere on the island.

There was no time to adjust to surroundings or find the way. At the arrival of the transport from Malino, Yamaji handed out a few clothes, and my mother was immediately set to work in one of the two major projects of the camp: the sewing rooms and the pigsties. The Japanese loved pork, and 500 pigs were shipped to Kampili; my mother was one of a team of ten women and two dozen young boys who were instructed to keep the pigsty spotless and feed the beasts. In all but name, it was slave labor.

The same was true of the sewing rooms that supplied the uniforms for the Japanese military.

The pork went to the army in Macassar, not a single morsel for the prisoners, but the food for the pigs came from the hotels and the officers' mess halls and was worth examining. Ignoring the bad smell, some valuable scraps were scavenged by the pig team. However, the open drains carrying off the waste presented a threat, as they were the perfect breeding grounds for flies.

And flies caused dysentery.

They became so overwhelming that even Yamaji had to admit he was bothered by the swarms. Of course, there was no insecticide, and so the commandant had the fine idea to order his prisoners to bring to his office a minimum of 100 killed flies every day. The women knew where to find them, and in great numbers, dashed off to the piggery to fill their quota. This scheme only ended when the pigs became noticeably agitated by the invasions and Yamaji got tired of counting dead flies.

The sewing rooms, established in August 1943 and extended a year later, were set up in two locations. One was of concrete, a small old storage room; the other one a bamboo barrack specially constructed for the purpose. The sewing machines, cloth, and sewing kits came from Macassar. It grew into a large enterprise in order to provide the military with the uniforms without disrupting the delivery chain. Well over 100 women were constantly employed at eighty sewing machines and at other equipment for buttonholes and the like. As usual, nothing was saved for the prisoners. They picked up leftover pieces from the floor and manufactured, one way or another, an outfit or two for themselves and their children.

The respective block heads handed out the chores around the camp on a rotating basis. My mother, although far from being a seamstress, naturally preferred the job in the sewing room to the piggery, away from odors, out of the sun, and in the wet monsoon, out of rain showers.

Camp life assumed a routine; the hardships were daily occurrences that required adaptation. The boys older than sixteen were separated from their families and shipped off to the men's camps. The latrines were, at times, dusted with lime. The latrines scared me; they were dark, flies buzzed, they were slippery, they smelled, but my mother insisted we use them. Other children would sometimes be negligent and mess things up outside. With intestinal worms and illnesses, this was far from beneficial to our health. When the dry monsoon changed into the wet monsoon, the rains came pouring down, causing our dirt floors in the barracks to become streams of red mud, not to speak of the mud and water around the barracks. Clothes that were worn during the outside jobs would not dry and simply rotted.

Each set of barracks had its own characteristics. It turned out that the complex with barrack eight was receiving more scrutiny than our number six, holding the ninety-two nuns and only Dutch women and children. Barrack eight was the one with the multiple nationalities and, above all, with the three American missionaries. It was not the missionary aspect that drew attention, it was the nationality of Japan's greatest enemy, America.

One day in April of 1944, officers of the Kempeitai showed up in shining black limousines. The entire camp held its breath. Yamaji had nothing to do with it; all the occupants of each and every camp all over the Pacific were registered in an elaborate numerical system by the Japanese Command in Tokyo. The Kempeitai were the secret police, well-schooled in torture, along the Bushido lines. These two officers came for the American women, accusing them of spying and hoarding money. The three missionaries were whisked off and not heard from again until four months later when they were returned to camp, emaciated, with hair gone white, sick, and one of them insane. Darlene Deibler writes about her ordeal in her book *Evidence Not Seen.*

The women had been incarcerated in Macassar in an insane asylum converted into a prison to be used by the secret police. They were tortured, had been secluded in solitary confinement in a six-foot square cell, went seventy-two hours without a bathroom stop while sick with dysentery, and had been given food spiked with worms. Yamaji was concerned about them and, every now and then, would go by the jail to check if there was any news. He managed to slip a banana or two by Darlene's cell, which gave her spirit and her stomach a boost. After their jail time, the women were left alone in Kampili and joined camp life again. For the missionary who had become mentally ill, there was no hope.

While the prisoners were at work, Peter, all the kids running around loose, and I were looked after by some of the nuns or mothers who had a few moments to spare. Discipline was not in the books. Once or twice, we were lined up and told: "Whatever you were doing; do not do it anymore," and subsequently dismissed. For the children, it was hard to know who our mother was; she was hardly ever there. At bedtime, the three of us had a few moments together. We would sit on the lower rack, and my mother would chat with us, or tell us a story, or hum a tune.

With one kerosene lamp in the middle of the barracks, the evenings and the dark nights were the times that my mother was most besieged with anxiety and loneliness. There was nothing to distract her; Peter and I were asleep and sheltered. Her thoughts would go back to light and joy or speed ahead to uncertainty and worries. She would go over the events of the day, analyzing the quarrels and arguments, the jealousy, the different personalities. But she also had friends, women who would look out for each other, women who shared stories, laughter, anxieties, sometimes even shared scraps of food or pieces of cloth. These few but precious friendships would last through the camp years and were enjoyed for many years after the war.

In general, however, a mood of dissension and discord hung over the camp, each woman reacting differently to the rigors of prison life. My mother realized she needed to cultivate passivity to stay out of arguments, which went directly against her strong, independent nature but, for her own good, she needed to learn. How long would this war last, how much longer would they be in captivity and subjected to illness, hunger, and dirt? She knew it was useless to ask why all of this was happening. If she just knew where her husband was, she would be less unhappy.

She bemoaned the lack of privacy she was forced to endure ever since she and her children had left Endeh. Even at night on her bunk, she was surrounded by people. But one thing stood out, above and beyond all her musings. She must stay alive for her children. When she passed the cemetery daily on her way to work, pausing at the graves, she wondered: Could she keep herself and her children alive? Would her children be able to grow not having enough food; would they suffer lifelong issues if they survived at all? There was sickness, ill health, and death everywhere she looked. She clearly remembered the first deaths; how many more would follow? One-third of the camp was sick with dysentery, the hospital was filled to the brim, the women in the last stages were closely watched during the night, as rats would emerge, smelling death and decay. Malaria was prevalent, another disease for which there were no drugs. Then there were the worms.

Children and adults were infested with roundworms, hook-worms, pinworms; children got bloated stomachs, for which there was no cure; sometimes a red onion, if available, was swallowed in chunks. Head lice were treated with a rag dipped in kerosene and tied around the head after all the hair had been cut off.

She watched the childless women give up battling the injustices, the illnesses, the hunger. She saw them deteriorate and, finally, succumb to depression and negligence. It occurred to her that mothers with children would fight and endure the hardships in order to keep their children alive. She understood that this determination was their own salvation, as well as a chance for their children to survive. My mother knew what to do, and Peter and I became her motivation to push ahead, not to give up. She resented the fact that she was deprived of the enjoyment of having her children, no nice outfits, no playfulness, and no cheer. Instead, what she was asked to do was to keep us from dying. The joy was stolen from her.

We were sick, like everybody else. My mother suffered recurrent bouts of malaria and Peter dysentery, black off and on, eliminating his innards, which my mother was required to push back in. I had worms and an extended tummy; I was blue around the mouth. I also experienced attacks of pure hysteria. When my hollering and screaming would not stop, my mother was fetched from where she was at work to see if she could calm me down. Nothing helped until Dr. Marseille and my mother decided on shock therapy.

They collected water from the kitchen drum in a small bucket, and when it had cooled, they gently pushed my head under once or twice. I snorted and coughed and when I came up, I had no time to cry, busy wiping my face. It was a barbarous treatment, but this was a concentration camp without child psychologists or medication. My mother and the doctor hugged me and assured me all was well. They returned the bucket to the kitchen drum, where they added it to the boiling water. These attacks happened several times, but somehow, I grew out of it for a while, until anxiety struck me again.

As children, we bonded and played our own invented games. But I, besides being inventive, was also inquisitive, for which one day I paid dearly. I was nosey and eager to see what all the buildings were about, where the pigs were. I saw chickens and even a few cows in the cow pasture, all the food and eggs destined for the Japanese in Macassar. I approached the central kitchen and noticed a big heap of what I thought was black sand and decided to climb the hill. But the heap that had looked so inviting proved to be a covered mount of fire hiding the red, hot ashes from the kitchen.

I can still recall the scream that emerged from my deepest recess, that hollow, deep, dark pit. My pinched, closed eyes looked into black space, fear was choking me, my feet were mean, biting monsters. I floated, and besides my burning feet, I had no body. Today, still, the discoloration on my ankles are the scars.

Frightened women in the kitchen lifted me out and went to call my mother. There was nothing that could be done for me. Dr. Marseille was able to procure some bandages to keep the flies off. Day after day, I sat on my bed rack, rocking back and forth, monotonously droning: "Water, water." I was in another world, all by myself, without any sense of time. It broke my mother's heart. But I healed.

The kitchen shift began work at four o'clock in the morning to start fires on bamboo sticks that perhaps would not ignite. Each day, the women had to haul ten gallons of water from the few water wells that were inconveniently located a distance away from the central kitchen to boil the rice and clean the vegetables.

The head of food distribution calculated what was needed to feed more than 1,600 people per day and informed Yamaji. Food arrived in sacks on big trucks that a so-called "coolie gang," of which my mother was sometimes a part, had to unload and carry through hot sand or mud puddles, depending on the season, to the kitchen, sacks of nearly sixty pounds. It ruined my mother's feet for life.

The women prepared meals in big drums; the smoke of the bamboo gave it a distinct flavor. Water required boiling; we were each given a ration of one soup ladle of drinking water a day. If my mother was not carrying sacks, she was assigned to the early kitchen shift, which she utterly disliked, not so much for the early hours but for the reason that it was the place where most of the fights occurred.

Food was what kept us alive; food was what made the good and the bad in characters surface; food moved the nasty tongues. "She is fatter than we are; she must have been pinching." It was very difficult to dole out the exact portions, 100 per barrack. The flatware in our family of three consisted of two spoons and a fork; we had two tin plates and an old tin can. We would either eat at the long crude tables and benches in the barrack set up as a dining hall or take our plates somewhere outside.

The food supply was never enough; clothing, also supplied by the Japs, was never enough either. Nor was soap, and toothpaste or toothbrushes were out of the question. My mother hung onto the few brushes she had packed in Endeh, which our family shared, sometimes with a leftover crumb of soap for a thorough cleaning.

There was no money in circulation. A few coins and bills hidden in the most improbable places made it possible to buy a little something from a vendor who risked his life approaching the fence to sell an item of incalculable value to the prisoners. A tiny amount of extra food could be purchased, a small piece of cloth, all clandestinely and dangerously. These audacious vendors, taking pity on the women, were sometimes able to sneak a message or two through the barbed wire from the prisoner of war camps in Macassar and surroundings, whose wives and children were in Kampili. One of the vendors had picked up a rumor in a prisoner of war camp that my father had arrived in Australia, but my mother always had her doubts; the rumor was too shaky.

Even though Yamaji was a brute, he also had another side. It could not have been easy for him to keep discipline. In his culture, the personal fate of a woman was totally immaterial. Being faced with hundreds of recalcitrant women, who on top despised him, must have been a constant source of irritation. He seemed a reformed man since his transfer from the men's camp of Pare Pare, where he was known and feared as a tyrant. He talked to the American missionaries and asked questions, but how the answers were processed was anybody's guess. The dysentery epidemic gravely concerned him. Besides his previous endeavor to kill the flies, he had high-risk areas, like the marshes, dusted with lime. He permitted the women to give the children, about 400 of them, lessons in a barrack that had been converted into a school room, which without books or writing material was quite a task. Fortunately, there were several teachers among the prisoners who remembered enough to impart some knowledge to their pupils. He forbade Japanese visitors to the camp to take any females with them for their brothels. When he foresaw that the supply of rice could be cut short, he annexed twenty-five acres of paddy fields from the local population and ordered the prisoners to learn how to cultivate them. In addition, they were told to clear the areas behind the camp of the tall sharp grass and turn these into one large vegetable garden for which he, Yamaji, would provide saplings.

The block heads pointed out to Yamaji that he should be truly upset that the monotony of the work and the stress of camp life were hampering the quantity and the quality of the projects he demanded to be done. Distraction in the form of entertainment would lift spirits and enhance the output, they insisted. It was a smart move, a talking point that was hitting home. Yamaji saw the reasonableness of the argument and promised to look into it.

Unexpectedly, one day, the women noticed a piano being moved into the camp and a small treadle organ, presumably meant for the nuns. It caused excitement, and in no time, groups were organized. A small choir was born and came under the baton of Olga, a Russian concert pianist married to a Dutchman who knew several music scores by heart. My mother joined the choir.

Little theatrical pieces were performed, which was not my mother's bailiwick; she preferred to sing. The nuns happily played hymns, enthusiastically supported by Pastor Spreeuwenberg. In the church barracks that were newly constructed, Yamaji allowed more Sunday services and evening prayers. He was curious about these strange expressions of a faith so alien to him. Rehearsals and choir practices took place in the evenings in the dining barrack by the light of a single kerosene lamp. More school barracks sprung up, to the delight of the teachers and their students. True, the newly found entertainment did raise the spirits somewhat, but it was questionable if it answered the original purpose of the suggestion to Yamaji, increasing the work output. This had never been the motive of the block heads, but their ruse worked.

The commandant's willingness to listen to the women and his concern for the three American missionaries jailed by the Kempeitai spared Yamaji the death sentence. After the war, the Australians took him into custody and handed him over to a Dutch military court on Java. Some of the Kampili women were witnesses and had his sentence commuted to seven years of jail time.

But he was unpredictable, had a very mean streak, and his anger could be aroused and vicious in one unexpected flash, something the women were well aware, and very afraid, of. His cane was always at the ready. He had been trained to hand out physical punishment; he did not know better. And when work did not progress as he wished, he would get furious, consequences to be expected.

An element of nasty surprise were the sudden air raids that began to occur in 1944. Yamaji brought natives in to dig open trenches to serve as shelters, about 100 yards from the campgrounds, a covered one for himself and his aide. Mostly at night, Allied planes would appear over Macassar, and bombs could be heard to explode again and again. Because Kampili was surrounded by airfields and military installations, the danger was not far away. What was all this activity about? Because of the camp's enforced isolation, there never was any news from the outside. What was happening to the men in the military camps? No one dropped any pamphlets, Red Cross packages never made it into the camp, stolen by the Japs, presumably, nor did any letters from home get through.

The alarm bell rang constantly, the ringer receiving her instructions from Yamaji. My mother would grab Peter and me, get hold of a bed mat, and rush to the shelter, dragging and helping us along. A scared Yamaji insisted on speed; slowing down deserved a beating.

On a clear night, my mother, as a distraction, would tell us to look way up at the Milky Way. All through the night, she anticipated the rising of the planet Venus, the bright morning star. The trenches were only seventeen inches wide, and to save space, the children were placed toe to toe. The adults could not lean back or move about. It was damp down there and, during the wet monsoon, the ditches were lined with puddles. Yet, wet dirt or not, they were our shelters. We spent several hours each night, sometimes even the entire night, in the ditches.

Of course, the health of the women and children deteriorated rapidly because of lack of sleep, dampness, and worry. The hospital reached capacity once more. All this time, work quotas were still required to be met, a very tall order. In solidarity, women took over jobs that others were too weak to perform; the main tasks were the ones in the kitchen and the vegetable garden. The air raids upset the routine and the kitchen shift served food whenever it was ready; in the evening, it brewed some coffee or tea to take along to the shelters.

In early 1945, the air raids increased; many more planes were flying over and extra shelters, with and without cover, were dug throughout the camp. Verbal messages whispered through the wired fence by brave locals, assured the women that their men had been transferred to different locations away from the bombings. There were a number of daytime raids; the night raids became even more frequent.

When a bomb exploded nearby, Yamaji ordered the prisoners to spend every night in the trenches. In a dogfight, a Japanese plane with its red sun painted on its side, was shot and came down in flames. With Yamaji nearby there were no expressions of delight. Night after night, even when it rained, the women and children sat in the trenches, awed by the spectacle of the Allied planes caught in the searchlights. The bombing campaigns filled the prisoners with hope and excitement. This was war; who was winning? How could they get any news? Would they be free any time soon? What was freedom going to be like? What kind of world would be awaiting them?

One day in June, they noticed little scraps of pamphlets that must have been dropped at night. Yamaji confiscated them right away, but just in time, the women pieced together and deciphered small sections. It was a cartoon of a gorilla-type Japanese with a text in several languages, indicating that the power of the beast had been broken. It brought some levity to the camp but still not much hope. One pamphlet that had been rescued and read before being handed over to Yamaji was of a faded orange, the color of the Dutch royal dynasty, and said that Queen Wilhelmina was back on the throne in the Netherlands. This implied that the war in Europe was over.

Still, the women dared not hope. Holland was far away; the war in the Pacific Rim was a different one. The raids continued. Large American planes flew overhead and dropped bombs in the area on the airfields that were close by. There was a sense that the camp was right in the middle of the danger zone. We spent long, sleepless nights in the shelters. A bomb exploded about 200 yards away; shards wounded a few women, and more shards were discovered later in the day. The danger was real.

July 17, 1945, was a bright and sunny day. The schoolchildren were in their barracks having their lessons; the women were out at their work stations. The noise of bombs striking Macassar and clouds of smoke going up in the distance had become familiar, albeit scary, scenes. My mother and her shift were working in the vegetable garden when they heard the drone of planes approaching and counted more than twenty.

"Allies!" they cheered.

However, they were uneasy. Planes flying overhead, bombs thrown in the vicinity, made them decide to return to their barracks. They had barely made it to camp when those same airplanes began to fly at low altitude, and to their total amazement, they saw the pilots drop a string of canisters.

Then they knew these were firebombs. Within seconds, the vegetable garden that my mother had just left was in flames; the shrieks of 500 pigs meant that the pigsty had also been hit. My mother, panic stricken, looked everywhere for Peter and me, calling our names repeatedly. She could not find us; she dashed to the shelters, fervently praying that we had been taken care of by one of our guardians. We were both found, and the three of us, close together, hunkered down, surrounded by other women and children who were as frightened as we were.

By intuition, my mother had selected one of the covered shelters, hoping for some protection. It proved to be the best choice; those in the open trenches had been hit hardest and were frightfully wounded. The planes returned. Wave after wave, they dropped their bombs. We stayed in the ditch, and when my mother peeked out, through thick smoke she saw women and children running around the camp, crazed, screaming, and without aim. Finally, the squadron disappeared, and this time, it did not return. When my mother dared to leave the trenches with us clinging to her, the barracks were in flames, we heard the roar of fires, heard the pops of bamboo bursting. The heat was intense. The smell of burned pigs and chickens was horrid. Together with all the other barracks, ours was gone; what little possessions we had were gone. The kitchen was partly demolished. Yamaji organized that the wounded were taken to Macassar. The women had the grim task of searching for the dead and taking care of the burials, assisted by Father Beltjens and Pastor Spreeuwenberg. Seven people perished, among them children.

Our camp is bombed and burned, searching for belongings

Not until after the war did we learn that we had been the victim of faulty intelligence. The Japanese had refused to mark our prison as a camp for women and children, and because of the location of airfields and military installations around Kampili, we were thought to be the enemy.

Somehow, my mother never found out how, Yamaji foresaw the possibility of a bombardment and assured that an emergency camp was constructed nearby in the woods, about a ten-minute walk, our new lodgings. It was a ramshackle collection of barracks built on short stilts, of very small proportion, barely able to accommodate the more than 1,600 women and children from Kampili. Insects crawled up the stilts and plagued us at night. The forest camp, which the Dutch called "Boskamp," had no water, no latrines; the prisoners had to go into the bushes. The women prepared meals in the ruins of Kampili's central kitchen and carried them in large tubs to the forest camp, as they did with our drinking water.

The bombardments on Macassar never ceased, and my mother had to take us out to the woods time and again for shelter. She pressed our heads into the damp forest floor in order to protect our ears from popping by the blasts, with the risk that we would hit leftovers of people's visits to the shrubs. We gagged, our mouths filled with dirt, but anything was better than ruined ears.

Nuns in Boskamp

July 19, 1945, was also a sunny day. My mother went to the old camp, taking us along, hoping against hope, to check if there was anything left of our possessions in the ruins of barrack number six. Nothing remained for her to retrieve. The camp was deserted, the hospital of concrete that was not destroyed, had been emptied out, and the patients transported to the dysentery barracks that were outside the campgrounds. A few women poked around in the ashes; a group of boys buried rotting pigs.

When they heard the distant hum of planes approaching again, it was not a good sound. My mother got hold of Peter and me and ran back to the emergency camp, just in time. Two more planes dropped heavy explosives and obliterated the few remaining concrete buildings, including the rest of the central kitchen barrack The women now had to cook food out in the open. Prisoners in the forest camp, scared to death, fled to the woods, hoping that the green canopy would render them unseen. When the bombing finally stopped, Kampili was totally ruined.

Life in the forest camp went on, although with no lessons, no more church services, no more plays or singing. The despair became palpable.

But Yamaji cheered us up, he thought, by promising that Kampili would be rebuilt. The war was still going on, he said, and the Japanese were going to be victorious; life would be good again.

6

Family Events

"When injustice becomes law, resistance becomes duty."
~ Thomas Jefferson (1743-1826)

In the camps all over the Pacific Rim, we lived under a totalitarian regime where victims had no certainty of decent treatment or even of survival. Survival depended entirely on the whimsicality of fate, which can hold destruction or death.

What happened to both Evert and his sister Dee, my father's siblings, is a case in point, as is the story of the woman Luut Ubels, a friend.

Evert left the Dutch Indies in his teens to finish school in the Netherlands, following it up with enrollment at the Institute for Business in The Hague. But when his fiancée died, he abandoned his studies and, in 1924, he returned, starting out as an employee with a large Dutch company in Padang on the island of Sumatra, whose main commerce was coffee and rubber.

A tall, handsome man, charming and outgoing, he remained a bachelor until 1927, when he asked the cousin of his deceased fiancée to join him. Tiddy (Johanna Varenkamp, born in 1906) arrived in due course, and they were married in 1928. They had two sons, Evert-Jan, born in 1929, and Michiel in 1941.

After a few years, the family moved from Sumatra to Java. Evert started work with the government in Batavia, in a subdivision of the Department of Economic Affairs, het Landbouw Syndicaat (agricultural syndicate), that dealt essentially with coffee. It was an important and influential organization that promoted the interests of the plantations and served as an advisory board to the government.

Evert's position with the syndicate was assured; his family enjoyed a comfortable life, although initially, the tropics were a cultural shock for Tiddy, who had never left Holland. She came around; what was there not to like about an abundance of flowers, fruits, fragrances, and servants? Like most people who returned to the Dutch Indies after an absence of a few years, Evert was happy to reunite with everything he remembered from his childhood. The tropics, the Indies, the fragrances, the colors were home.

When the Japanese conquered Java in March 1942, they allowed the syndicate to continue its work, possibly at the suggestion of a Japanese agronomist at the syndicate, Naruzawa, who had lived on Java for the last seventeen years. While at work, the Dutch employees were not averse to sabotage, helping people with money, as bank accounts were frozen, and supporting a resistance movement that was born in the hills of West Java.

In January 1943, the Kempeitai presented the members of the syndicate with a petition that ordered them to pledge loyalty to the Japanese command and to betray those people they suspected of subversive activities. Seventeen employees refused to sign the document, which they called "The Oath of Betrayal." One of them was Evert. He had a sense of justice that would never allow for similar actions. All was quiet for a few months while the Kempeitai and the Japanese of the syndicate argued as to whether or not to let the refusal to sign stand.

The Kempeitai won.

In July, fourteen men were arrested, and on August, 27, two women were also taken into custody. Sixteen employees of the syndicate were imprisoned in the notorious jail of Batavia.

The seventeenth person, Luut Ubels, had her own story and appointment with fate. She was born in 1919 and since 1936 had been employed by a branch office of the syndicate until July 1943, when she was dismissed.

On the same day, August 27, 1943, that the two syndicate women were taken into custody, a Kempeitai officer arrived at the house of the family Ubels with an arrest warrant for L. Ubels, surprised to find a woman. By that time, the Ubels family had already suffered many tragedies. In the first days of the Japanese occupation, son Jan had gone missing, another son was a prisoner of war in a camp south of Bandung, and in May, Father Ubels, a protestant minister, was apprehended and incarcerated. Son Lambert, nicknamed Sam, not quite yet seventeen, was all of a sudden the eldest man in the house.

For the time being, the mother and the two children, Luut and Lambert, remained in the parsonage. A friend of the family got Lambert a job with the earlier mentioned Landbouw Syndicaat.

His employment set the wheels of fate in motion. Sam stayed with the syndicate for about seven months until it was his turn to be fired, but not before he, too, refused to sign the petition. A few weeks later, they interned him, luckily in the same camp as his father, whom he could provide with extra bits of food he pinched as a kitchen aid. He was totally unaware of the tragic outcome regarding the petition.

When the doorbell rang, with Sam imprisoned, Luut remained the last sibling left in the parsonage. She was summoned to pack a small suitcase and to come with the officer. Both mother and daughter were left with the question of how long she would be away? Only a few days maybe, or perhaps for the duration of the war.

But Luut did not come home, and nothing was ever heard from her again. Had the Kempeitai confused the names of herself and her brother, both beginning with "L"?

After their arrest, the prisoners had one more chance to sign the nefarious petition, which again all of them refused to do, this time including Luut, who had not seen the document before. One wonders if they fully understood the consequences of their action.

By then, in prison, Luut may have realized that hers was a case of mistaken identity. It was her brother Lambert, as a signatory of the petition, whom the Kempeitai was after. If so, she must have maintained her silence and taken her brother's place.

Evert did not return, nor did Luut, nor did the other prisoners.

There is a cemetery on the way from Batavia to the harbor named Ancol. After the war, a deaf mute guard of a nearby Chinese temple explained in sign language to the caretakers of the graves that he knew what had happened under the single tree on the grounds, at that time no more than a mangrove. Here, in the swamp, the Japanese executed hundreds of people in the name of the emperor. But it was under this tree, he signaled, that on September 23, 1943, they executed fourteen men and three women. With his own eyes, he explained, he witnessed how, in true Japanese fashion, they were decapitated; his sign language probably accentuated it with a gesture across his throat.

This is how Evert and the other captives ended their lives. It was assumed that the third woman beheaded was Luut. It would be a fair conclusion. Not having received a word from her since the day the Kempeitai officer appeared at her home, as well as her connection, although distant, with the syndicate, would be reasonable indicators, but doubts have always remained.

While in Indonesia, my brother Peter visited Ancol several times and stood by the white crosses bearing Evert's name, as well as the names of the other syndicate victims. It was a meticulously kept, quiet cemetery. All the graveyards, spread out over Java and the Far East, are permanently and impeccably tended by the Dutch War Graves Committee.

Evert Neeb

Luut Ubels

After the war, in 1947, at the temporary Military Tribunal in
Batavia, witnesses, Sam was one of them, gave their testimonies
regarding crimes committed by the Kempeitai. According to Sam,
the arrest and the execution of his sister were a flagrant injustice; the
Kempeitai had neglected to properly investigate the case of L. Ubels.
The conclusion of the witnesses was that Luut Ubels had pled guilty
to save her brother's life. Sam was, in a special way, forever connected
with the death of his sister. The children of the syndicate victims,
including Evert's sons Michiel and Evert-Jan, stayed in touch for
some time after the war. But, as they felt there was nothing to gain
from their relationships, they went their separate ways. And so, the
question as to how Sam coped with the sacrifice of his sister was
never answered.

When the United States learned of the Japanese practice of
decapitating prisoners without due process in contravention of the
Treaties of Geneva regarding prisoners of war, which the Japanese
had signed but never ratified, they threatened to kill ten Japanese
people living in America for every Allied prisoner executed.

This sounded better than it was, as the Japanese continued to behead their captives nonstop while no Japanese person in the United States was ever reported to have been killed in retaliation. It would have been easy enough for the Americans to locate them since 110,000 Japanese-Americans from the three western coasts had been rounded up and interned in government constructed settlements in the desert of California.

Because the forces of Imperial Japan in early 1942 rapidly occupied vast areas of the Pacific, combined with the known spy activities of the Japanese-born citizens in Hawaii and California, the Roosevelt administration deemed it wise to seclude the innocent and not-so-innocent Japanese in areas far from potential war activities, aware that blood runs a lot thicker than water. Although these people had to cope with the loss of freedom, way of life, and had to give up properties and possessions, their seclusion was in no way comparable to the satanic tyranny suffered by the Caucasians at the hands of the Japanese captors during their incarceration. Their circumstances were admittedly unenviable, but the Nissei never had to confront the histrionics of the Imperial army, nor were they starved to death, tortured, or beaten beyond recognition.

When Tiddy and her two boys ended up in Camp Tjideng near Batavia, Evert was still at work at the syndicate. Tjideng was unlike our camp in Kampili; we were put up mainly in barracks of bamboo and straw. Tiddy's camp consisted of appropriated homes surrounded by barbed wire located in one of the suburbs. It held well over 10,000 women and children. It was an abysmal place, overcrowded and run by Commandant Sunei, a manic depressive who was drunk most of the time and suffered from moon sickness, when he would go totally berserk. After his rages, he dressed up in his finest and pretended nothing had ever occurred.

Michiel, just a toddler born a few months before my brother Peter, and Evert-Jan, together with their mother, suffered the same indignities, brutality, hunger, and illness as all of us did in each and every camp, with the exception that their commander was unusually brutal. He received the death sentence at the Tokyo War Crimes Trial and was executed, never showing remorse; it had all been for the emperor. Tiddy turned completely deaf in the camp. Evert-Jan, at that time thirteen years old, was moved to a boys' cum men's camp and back again to Tjideng. The reason behind the transfers is obscure. The fate of these boys, separated in the women's camps from their families at about that age, was ugly as in their new surroundings they were subjected to rape and other molestations by the Japs. Could that have happened to Evert-Jan?

Tjideng held the dubious distinction of being the worst of all of the civilian camps in the Dutch East Indies under the reign of terror of Sunei. During their entire incarceration, Tiddy and her sons were unaware of the events at the syndicate and at Ancol.

Until well after the war, nobody in the family knew what had happened at the syndicate. It was only in October of 1945 that my grandpapa, who had been searching all this time for his kin, found out how, where, and when his son was executed.

The destiny of Evert was to pay with his life for his rebellion and sense of justice. His sister Dee, equally rebellious and righteous, was confronted with a different trick of fate.

While my mother, Peter, and I were in our camp at Kampili on the island of Celebes, and Tiddy and her sons in Tjideng near Batavia on Java, the other members of the family, although not fixed in camps, faced their own fair share of exposure to Japanese atrocities. Grandmama and Grandpapa Neeb lived in Bandung with their daughter Dee, son-in-law Gerard Kloosterhuis, and their small granddaughters, Lily and Edith.

The Japanese arrived on Java and moved into Bandung by the middle of March 1942, which signaled the end of a sweet life with servants and creature comforts. Bandung, in the hills, enjoys a moderate climate and is surrounded by nature in all its glory, botanical gardens, rice fields, cool mountains.

But, with the occupation, the Japanese confiscated homes, relocated people to different houses, all cramped together, or threw them into camps that were erected in and around the town. They crowded Dee and her family into a house with several floors and with too many people per floor.

At first, the family managed to stay out of the camps and confinement for a while. My grandpapa was smart; he had found a loophole in the distribution of identity cards. The Japanese considered anyone who was of the third generation born in the Dutch Indies as Indonesian, and therefore, not eligible for incarceration. My grandpapa set out to prove that this was the case with his family since they had arrived a long time ago, in the 1860s. Thus, the family's passes were properly stamped "Belanda-Indo 3," belanda stood for white or "Hollander," the indo was the designation for the Asian population, which kept them out of the camps, the "3" indicated "third generation." This did not mean life was easy. Like all around the archipelago, food was scarce, restrictions on movement were imposed, medication was a luxurious commodity, houses were overcrowded, the obligatory bowing to any Japanese encountered was deeply humiliating.

My grandpapa, as a mining engineer, constructed some type of shelter from pieces of wood inside the house they were allocated in case of an air raid. Dee took pity on the local women and girls inside and outside the camps. To keep them out of the brothels, she started a knitting and sewing group to provide the army with socks and underwear. She received the yarn and cloth from the Japanese who were quite pleased with this productivity and allowed the knitting circles to continue.

Of a more dangerous nature were Dee's bicycle rides, when she regularly smuggled food and fruit into the camps and sometimes even some money that she had hidden at the beginning of the war. Besides activities that were relatively in sight, Dee and my grandpapa were also involved in underground work, resisting the Japs when they could. For one thing, they protected a Dutch family that had hidden a radio and could listen to news from Australia. When a Kempetai officer dropped by for an inspection, Dee used to show him tuberculosis sputum from a sick Chinese man nearby as the reason the family was in hiding, scaring the officer off.

Concealing their activities couldn't last. In spite of their stamp of "Belanda-Indo 3," in June of 1944, my grandpapa and Dee were arrested. One member of the group had been apprehended, probably after a radio signal was detected, and during a bloody Kempeitai interrogation, he had folded and given, among others, the names of my grandpapa and Dee, mentioning Dee as the leader of the group. My grandpapa was seventy-five years old; Dee was forty-two.

My grandpapa was equipped with a well-developed survival instinct. Daily he practiced the bit of yoga he remembered from his long-ago visit to Tibet, instructing his cellmates to do the same. He knew that the food in the hospital section of the jail was better than his cell food and made sure he had frequent bouts of severe diarrhea by eating the wrong fruit so he could be admitted to the hospital, as well as to a bed that was more comfortable than the narrow cot he had in his cell. It was never quite clear what cell food consisted of; the inmates suspected rats, and snakes, and worms, and dog meat, and the like. My grandpapa must have become used to this staple since he needed to chew a special kind of nut to make him sick enough for the hospital ward.

At first, Dee was in the same prison as her father, subjected to Kempeitai torture for more disclosures. She refused to give any names and was transferred to a prison in Batavia with instructions to the military tribunal to condemn her to death.

One day, after her sentence, she was in her cell when the Japanese executioner came by and spoke to her through the barred window. "You are first on my list tomorrow." Dee was a very cultured woman and had read a lot in her life and especially, living in Asia, about Japan and Japanese culture. She was also fearless. She addressed the guard and asked him how long it took a Samurai to become proficient in neatly executing a decapitation with one big slash of the sword. The guard answered he was not allowed to divulge any Samurai secrets and would not tell her. She insisted, "I will keep your secret; I am giving you my word. Besides, you just told me what I can expect tomorrow." She was clearly taunting him.

The next morning, the same guard was at her window, completely crazy, yelling at her beside himself, rattling the bars hysterically. She was grateful to be on the safe side of his madness. It turned out that, miraculously, she had been removed from the death list, and although she had promised she would never betray him, he knew that in order to defend his honor, he had to commit *hara-kiri* and fall on his sword. Dee enjoyed the satisfaction of knowing she had caused the Japanese Imperial Army to lose one of its fine soldiers. Because her sentence was commuted, she was transferred to yet another prison, this time to Semarang on the north coast of Java.

By purely a twist of fate, she had survived the sword, and Evert had not. For her bravery, Dee received a decoration; Evert was decorated posthumously.

Gerard, Dee's husband, was often called away from the house to pursue his profession as a doctor. Like my father, he served as a medical officer in the army. Before long, he did not come home, and the family learned he had been arrested and put into a camp nearby. The girls were allowed to visit him but barely recognized their father behind the barbed wire among the men with shaven heads.

Gerard had the misfortune that at this time in history he happened to be an army officer, for like all military forces, he was destined to become a prisoner of war. The POWs, for short, were the recipients of the strictest form of Bushido with all its barbarity. The soldiers were brutally treated as contemptible specimens, for they had allowed themselves to be captured. The Samurai code extolled courage, loyalty, and bearing the unbearable, qualities which in their view captured soldiers were pitifully lacking. They were no more than a subhuman species.

This was the basis of the difference between the POW camps and the civilian camps operated by the Japanese. The POW camps contained soldiers who had surrendered; they were, therefore, considered cowards, despicable and deserving of death. Their treatment was, without exception, sadistic. Although in the civilian camps the Japs kept non-military persons under strict surveillance and control by humiliating, starving, and beating them, the way these prisoners were treated was still in no way comparable to the appalling, maniacal behavior of the Japanese guards toward their POW-prey, incomprehensible to those who did not experience it.

While in Australia, my father found the names of Gerard and his old friend and colleague from Timor, Dr. Hekking, on a list of prisoners in a POW camp in Thailand. The Dutch arrived there in February of 1943. My father was not aware that this was the forced labor camp charged with the building of one of the bridges over the Mae Klong River on the Burma-Thailand Railroad at the village of Tamarkan. The Japanese had conquered Burma and Thailand and needed a supply route from Rangoon to Bangkok; the ocean route infested with torpedoes was too dangerous. For the railroad, they recruited nearly 11,000 slave laborers. This bridge is made famous by the Hollywood movie, *The Bridge over the River Kwai*, a production, unfortunately, that was more fiction than fact.

British Lt. Col. Philip Toosey commanded the camp and was not afraid to stand up to his Japanese captors. But he faced a problem. The Japanese planned to build the railroad, no matter what, however sick the men were. They dismissed Geneva Convention rules regarding the treatment of prisoners; a dead body could easily be replaced from the pool of thousands of prisoners. The colonel gave his men a pep talk, warning them to be cooperative and cheerful, knowing full well that when push came to shove, the Japs were the winners.

In spite of Toosey's up-beat speech, the prisoners soon realized that their captors were all powerful and had no scruples exercising that power. The inhuman conditions forced the men into solidarity, which at the same time probably increased their chances of survival; lasting friendships were made. When they labored on the bridges, with the most primitive tools and pulleys, the guards constantly harassed and beat them using corporal and violent punishment from the Bushido manual. The Kempeitai would visit the camp, armed with a selection of torture tools and instructions as to how best to conduct an interrogation.

Ignoring the threat of punishments and expressions of sadism hanging over their heads, the prisoners sabotaged their construction in any way they could imagine, even inserting white ants and termites into the wooden structures. Their days were long; they were usually on their feet more than ten hours in the scorching, tropical sun. Sometimes they were provided with kerosene lamps to continue work after dark. Food consisted of the starvation-diet variety, prepared on an open wood fire on a flat stone. Gerard kept his mess tin, spoon, and knife until the end of his day.

The work, the punishments, the insufficient food, the exposure to threats from the jungle naturally led to untold cases of ailments and deaths. The hospital was no more than a bamboo hut without mattresses, sheets, or pillows with three doctors and one or two surgeons who had no instruments or medication to speak of. The Dutch of the East Indies knew about tropical ulcers and the devastating diseases but were not prepared for the inhumane conditions they met.

The doctors needed to invent new remedies and methods. With their knowledge of the tropics and its maladies, they were familiar with the medicinal propensities of herbs, leaves, and grasses. Dr. Henri Hekking was the motor and was able to guide his team through the labyrinth of herbal medicine. Born and raised on Java, he had learned from his mother and grandmother the value of herbs from the forests. With his refined jungle medicine, he was able to save many lives. But still, amputations needed to be performed without anesthetics, wounds and ulcers were scraped with scalpels, and medicines were concocted at Dr. Hekking's shed, together with new discoveries by the members of the doctor's team.

The Allied aircraft attacked the bridge as well as the railroad several times, destroying gauges and one span of the steel bridge at Tamarkan. The camp was hit time and again. Not much was left and several prisoners were killed. By February 1945, the Japanese decided to proceed with evacuation and move the remaining prisoners to Camp Chungkai two miles up north. Conditions improved slightly, but camp life, with its arbitrary punishments and customary deficiencies, was not over yet.

Parallel with the predicament of the Japanese-American population in the United States ran the situation of the Germans in the Dutch East Indies. After Hitler's armies invaded Holland in May 1940, their compatriots in the Indies were considered enemies of the state and forthwith interned in Soerabaja on Java. Approximately 2,800 Germans, among them Nazi sympathizers, young, old, Jewish, missionaries, engineers, doctors, women, and children were captured, their properties confiscated. It was unjust internment; not even half of the group could be classified as pro-Germany.

Karel Raedt van Oldenbarnevelt, as a civil servant with the government, was charged with tracking down the pro-Germans. He had his eyes on a certain Colonel Meyer who was known to be a member of the Dutch party that was sympathetic to the Nazis. However, Meyer managed to turn the tables and branded Karel as a Nazi sympathizer. Among the original 2,800 prisoners, there were 146 Germans, as well as Dutch, who were deemed the most fervent sympathizers, and therefore, the most dangerous individuals. Under the command of Colonel Meyer, they were shipped from Soerabaja to Surinam, a Dutch colony situated on the north coast of South America. The voyage took forty days in an iron cage, burning hot, underneath the deck of the ship, a sordid warning of what could very well lie ahead. Their destination was a camp about forty miles south of the capital city of Paramaribo, named the "Joden Savanne" (Savanna of the Jews), an old, abandoned sugar plantation in the jungle that in the late 1600s was cultivated by Sephardic Jews from Spain. They disappeared a long time ago, after persecution and subsequent dispersion.

The Dutch marines, together with the Surinam guards, meted out the same types of punishment to their 146 prisoners as was customary in prisoners' camps. There was brutality, no hygiene, no food, no medicine, the inmates subjected to heavy, forced labor. This was all the more disturbing coming from Dutch marines to some of their own nationals, Nazi-sympathizers or not, and smacked, among other things, of retaliation for the German occupation of the Netherlands.

Conditions in the camp were so appalling that Colonel Meyer saw a chance to display a show of pity for some of his charges. Feigning compassion, he offered van Oldenbarnevelt and a fellow prisoner the chance to escape. It was Meyer's fiendish plot, his revenge. While both prisoners were on the run, he had them shot and killed in the back, a tried and true trick.

Van Oldenbarnevelt was forty-seven years old.

The behavior of the Dutch marines in Surinam was far from their finest hour. Yet curiously, after the war, the Netherlands government made no effort to put them on trial, their deplorable actions were not examined. Neither did the judicial system investigate the outright murders of van Oldenbarnevelt and his fellow inmate. It seemed that the philosophy was to let bygones be bygones. Van Oldenbarnevelt's widow emigrated to Australia.

The shrewd and disreputable Colonel Meyer returned to Java at war's end to fight the guerillas of the Indonesian independence forces. For his contribution to the battle, he received the highest Dutch military decoration. When, finally, rumors and initial investigations began to surface, Meyer post haste emigrated to the United States, acquired American citizenship, and thus, remained untouchable.

7

Deliverance

"The war has developed not necessarily to Japan's advantage."
~ Hirohito, Emperor of Japan (1901–1989)

The air over the Pacific Rim was one of putrefaction. Wherever the Japanese had put their boots down, there was death and destruction. The same was true and never changed in the camp near Kampili where my mother, Peter, and I still lingered.

Pencil drawing of Boskamp by my mother's friend Magda Buffart

Our jungle camp, "het Boskamp," was a miserable, primitive place without water, latrines, or eating barracks. Jungle insects crawled everywhere. Especially at night, the women and children were unprotected and bitten by mosquitoes and other bugs, carriers of more illness. At times, they spotted gruesome monitor lizards. Tubs of food and buckets of water needed to be carried down continuously from the old, burned camp, where one or two wells still functioned.

Peter and I were sick with dysentery, and my mother suffered from after-effects of malaria. Under the deteriorating conditions in which we were forced to live, our survival became a matter of touch-and-go. Courage and perseverance in the camp rapidly dissolved. Far too many people were stacked up in one place and with the lack of sanitary facilities the situation became practically unlivable. My hysterical attacks returned, and my mother saw no other remedy than the one she and Dr. Marseille had practiced earlier. She carefully immersed my head again in a precious bucket of water. Once more, the method proved effective, especially when I received my mother's attention with soothing words and reassurances. For our meals, we squatted in the sand and dirt, and when people walked by, dust settled onto our plates. Flies came after our food; my mother continuously waved her hands so we would not swallow a collection of insects.

As Yamaji had promised, work was underway at the old Kampili camp to rebuild the barracks. Trucks loaded with bamboo and construction equipment came and went. The women were not at all eager to relocate since a new camp would mean a continuation of imprisonment and war.

But there were signs, hopeful ones even. Planes continued to throw their bombs in the area, and a positive tiding about the war's progress was picked up from a local vendor brave enough to approach the fence. A name went around the camp, "Truman, who is Truman?" As the sewing room in Kampili had begun production again, although on a very limited scale because the replacements of the burned sewing machines were slow in coming, cloth was dropped off at the camp.

This time, it was not the usual army khaki material but cotton in pleasant colors. Then tennis shoes made it into the camp, a messy heap since they were not in pairs, hundreds of them. But paired or not, they were more than welcome, sorting them out was a joyful task. It was all rather bewildering. Moreover, it so happened that Yamaji could not hold his tongue, and perhaps entirely inadvertently, and cryptically, said to a few women: "I will take care of you until the Americans come."

One day, it was August 15, 1945, the feared black limousine of the Kempeitai drove into the camp. Hearts stopped, "Whose turn was it this time?" But Yamaji got into the car and left, to return a few hours later.

The next day, August 16, Yamaji left again in a black car, this time accompanied by the head of the camp, Mrs. Joustra. It was all so mysterious, the women were convinced this meant another transfer to another terrible camp until Kampili was finally reconstructed. When, after two hours, Yamaji and Mrs. Joustra returned, the message went around that everybody, young and old, including ambulatory patients, had to assemble on the large meadow in the old camp at exactly two-thirty in the afternoon. Soon Yamaji arrived with Father Beltjens, Pastor Spreeuwenberg, and Mrs. Joustra in tow. Yamaji wore his full uniform. One could hear a pin drop; there was total silence. What was going on?

Yamaji began to read a text in Malay but was unable to continue. All he could stammer, overcome with emotion, were four words: "Perang abis, lain tidak," which means, "The war is over, that is all." He walked away after his announcement and probably locked himself up in his office. Why had they lost the war in spite of their fanaticism, in spite of their vows to fight to the death?

Mrs. Joustra continued in Dutch, loudly, so her voice could be heard as far as the last rows. She told us about her ceremonial reception by the Japanese command in Macassar who said to her in Japanese, which was then translated into Malay, then translated again into English, that all over the Pacific the hostilities had ceased, Japan had surrendered. Across the entire Pacific Rim, soldiers laid their weapons down.

We were free; it was liberation; it was peace; the camp years were over.

My mother remembered how the silence continued. She heard a few sobs, but because for three and a half years the women had been drained of their emotions, there were none left for this huge event. Dumfounded, they stood around in the meadow, not sure what to do next. But after a while, Peter and I heard women sing, including my mother, who explained it was the Dutch national anthem, whatever that was.

Yet, my mother was sad, and she was terrified. Where was her husband? Did she have to go it alone? What was there on the outside? What happened to the family? Where was everybody? How could she find them? Where were clothes? Where was money? How sick were we? But, thank God, unbelievably, here we were, still a family of three, together. We had survived. There had been thirty-seven deaths in Kampili; seven had died in the bombing raid; fourteen of the dead were children.

Mrs. Joustra spoke again. Because nothing had been prepared in Macassar for our release, we were to remain in the camp. Some of the women would be moved, as space allowed, to the few finished barracks in Kampili. Yamaji would stay on, ironically, this time as our protector to maintain order. Within a week, the military hospital in Macassar would be made available for the patients of the sick ward of Kampili and of all the other camps in the area, the POW-camp of Macassar and the men's camp of Pare Pare. These instructions were only preliminary until Japanese rule could be handed over to the Netherlands Indies Civil Administration, or NICA.

The three of us stayed in the jungle camp, where conditions had improved considerably, not in the least because of the food droppings. An American naval officer had been signaled at the main camp, talking to women. He asked what they needed most and where would be a good dropping place. Together they decided that the meadow of the Kampili camp and a rice paddy field nearby would do very well. Yamaji ordered that some white cloth be delivered, and strips were torn for demarcation.

There the planes came: American planes, Australian planes, Dutch planes, nonstop, flying low, dropping parachutes with containers full of products we had not seen for a long time or even knew existed. The excitement of items falling from the skies, time and again, made the children shriek for joy and run all over the meadow. Women collected the goods and carried them to one specific place to be evenly distributed later. Cans of sweet condensed milk, tins of Spam, cereals, chocolates, bags of soap and combs, and more toiletries lay strewn all over the grass.

I tasted too much condensed milk and was sick. My mother warned us to go slowly on all the fine treats; our stomachs were in no shape to handle much food, as I had just shown. Fresh clothes were delivered from Macassar, as well as shoes. Seamstresses from outside the camp made dresses in the new sewing room installed in one of the finished barracks.

Reconstruction of the Kampili camp continued. Four of the sixteen barracks were completed; more would follow. We awaited the results of negotiations between the Allies and the Japanese, as well as the definitive signing of the peace accords in Japan. We should remain in the camp for about two more months, perhaps even longer, we were told. Administrative mills grind slowly. Macassar was not ready yet to receive us; there was not enough accommodation, not enough food and not enough protection.

Women with nursing or administrative skills left for Macassar immediately, as they were needed sorely. In the meantime, NICA contacted every type of organization to locate families spread out over the Pacific Rim and hopefully bring them together. The Red Cross proved a formidable source of information. On August 18, 1945, the Recovery of Allied Prisoners of War and Internees, RAPWI, was founded, which became a big part of the search.

It was the end of August. In the camp, we still waited for total peace. So far, it was the cessation of hostilities that had brought about our liberation, but the treaty had not been signed yet, and peace was still not official. My mother, Peter, and I remained in the dirty, primitive jungle camp but had more freedom of movement and could visit Kampili any time for a little diversion. We were instructed to wait while events beyond our control unfolded. But dysentery continued in the jungle camp. A lot of dust, a lot of flies, and deplorable hygiene caused more and more illnesses for the totally weakened and exhausted women and children.

Surprisingly, on September 2, seriously ill patients were transferred to the hospital in Macassar. Everything, all these years, had always occurred, and apparently continued to occur, without a previous warning or message. News would always be gathered at the fence from a vendor, or lately from torn up, hardly readable leaflets.

On September 4, a Dutch airplane flew over our jungle camp, just barely missing the top of the trees. It dropped off messages that we were able to figure out. My mother gratefully learned that the plane would fly over again the next day and drop additional medicine, vitamins, and food. More planes followed, including one with food and leaflets from the Royal Australian Airforce: "Chin up; we will be back," and suggested we send signals with mirrors about our needs, but nobody in the camp mastered this art. The signals would have been superfluous anyway; day in and day out, planes circled over our camp, and parachutes came down dropping crates with medicines, vitamins, bandages, Band-aids, dried fruit, toiletries.

For my mother, these were her most emotional moments. To know that after all these years of neglect and brutality, there were people out there wishing us well, reaching out to us, and wanting the best for us was almost too much to absorb.

The days dragged on, made easier by the airplanes and the parachutes with their delicacies. The three of us stayed in the jungle camp until mid-September.

In the meantime, one of the planes had dropped off a newspaper in English. This is how we learned that the war had officially ended with a signing ceremony on September 2, 1945, in Tokyo Bay on the Battleship *Missouri*. Since August 15, the day of surrender, we had waited. If it hadn't been for the English language paper, we would not have learned about the events in Japan. Besides that, more than a week went by after the document signing before we knew the war was officially over. But we were being fed, and we received clothing and shoes.

One day, it finally happened. A car came to pick us up and take my mother, Peter, and me to Macassar. It turned out that my father had been the magician, pulling strings behind the scene, getting us out of Kampili at liberation, making sure we had adequate accommodation. Through the Red Cross lists and RAPWI, through his numerous contacts, he had never given up his search and had finally located us.

What had brought Asia to this memorable point in history was the determination of the Americans and their Allies to bring down the monstrous regime that had reduced the captives to slaves. For years the war in the Pacific to restore freedom had been continuing unabated. The bloody campaigns to capture Okinawa and Iwo Jima stemmed from the plan to use the islands as staging areas for an invasion of Japan itself. On Okinawa, 12,520 American troops were killed.

Despite their immense losses in lives and equipment, the masses of Japanese military and civilians refused to believe that they were losing the war. The home front could not accept that the country had sustained great losses of military personnel and that its once formidable navy was now mostly on the bottom of the sea. The Japanese military, inspired by the romantic grip of the Bushido code, would fight an invading enemy to the last drop of blood and could never imagine that it might be defeated. As for the Americans and their Allied military leaders, the conflict with the fanaticism of the Japanese was recognized but did not necessarily discourage them while they contemplated an occupation of the home islands.

American airplanes had carried on saturation bombings over Japan for well over two years, but there was virtually no evidence that the Japanese were losing their will to carry on the war. Moreover, POWs, American, British, Australians, New Zealanders, and Dutch, were forcibly recruited into hard labor in Japanese armament plants and other public works. They would be the first to suffer from an Allied invasion, next of course, to the Japanese civilians.

The United States' naval officials agreed on a major attack on the southern island of Japan, Kyushu, in June 1945, but as the appointed date drew near, President Truman and his staff changed their mind, believing that the atomic bomb, now available, would create a greater incentive to surrender than just a military invasion of the home islands, leading to the loss of innumerable lives. Furthermore, it seems that Truman's inner circle was aware of Japan's plans to exterminate all

Western internees, military and civilian, on August 27. They were deadly serious unless the Allies would cease all hostilities. Relevant documents have surfaced in erstwhile Japanese headquarters in the Philippines, Singapore, and Bangkok and also in the United States. Besides, Japan calculated that it would win the war, and therefore upon its victory would be burdened with untold masses of white people.

Truman called Japan's bluff and used the atomic bomb, first on Hiroshima on August 6, and when there still was no sign of conciliation on the part of the Japanese, a second bomb was dropped on Nagasaki on August 9. After the attacks, the Japanese Foreign Ministry sent word to the United States that Japan was prepared to negotiate, however, with the understanding that the prerogatives of his majesty the emperor as sovereign ruler were not compromised.

In short, the Japanese hoped to bargain that the emperor would retain the old order. That same old order had recently launched a war of aggression that killed a minimum of seventeen million people. Japan clearly did not see its situation as hopeless.

President Truman and his general staff rejected the proposition immediately. The word was unconditional surrender.

Thus, the Battleship *Missouri* received its place in history on September 2, 1945, surrounded by an armada of cruisers with Japanese cabinet ministers and military officials on board and General Douglas McArthur and several other generals of the Allied armies as signatories. The ship was the scene of the official signing ceremony of the instrument of surrender, without terms attached, of the Empire of Japan. Emperor Hirohito listened to the proceedings on his radio in the palace.

Macassar had been bombed beyond recognition. When the car finally came for us in the Boskamp by mid-September, the three of us were taken to a hotel. My mother, Peter, and I slept in a queen-sized bed, with sheets, after nearly four years. Peter, fascinated with the WC and its chain, begged my mother: "Mom, may I please ring the bell again?"

In Macassar, in this hotel, after nearly four years, my mother saw her husband again, and we met a strange man who was our father. He was blond, big, and tall. Peter and I were intimidated, the only men we ever saw had been short and black-haired, with oval eyes and bowlegs. We were very shy and reluctant to embrace him, but it was clear to us that my mother was happy we were together again. He brought some clothes and some toiletries.

The next day, my father had to return to Australia for duty; he was still an army officer. It turned out we were brought together by a friend of my father's in Australia who was a pilot in the army, Hugo Haje. He had made it his hobby to reunite families, no matter how spread out they were, by skirting every bit of red tape, including the lists of the Red Cross and RAPWI that were made up of priority mobilizations. Without him, we would have been held up even longer in our dirty jungle camp. By chartering planes and using influential contacts, in order to avoid the numerous official channels, he helped many of his friends. After the war, Haje emigrated to California, where he got a job dusting crops from a small airplane. We were sad to learn that on one of his missions, the plane crashed and he was killed. He was our benefactor.

All the ex-prisoners, civilians and military, were divided over the European homes in four sections of what was left of the town of Macassar: one section for the Caucasians, one for the Indonesians, one for the Allied troops, and one for the Japanese. The houses were dirty, nothing worked properly, no windows could be closed, nor cabinets or doors, but there was water, there was electricity, and for the ex-internees, this was pure luxury. The local authorities distributed meals from one or two central kitchens. We could obtain clothing from a charity distribution that had confiscated all of the new army clothes from the Japanese. People went around town in every type of khaki outfit.

The streets were still crowded with Japanese soldiers. Trucks drove back and forth. The Japs were obviously moving somewhere, loaded up with mattresses and stolen furniture for some far-away or close-by destination.

When my mother saw all this activity, with her heart in her shoes, she knew it to be the fate of the household goods and mementos she had stored with the nuns. She lost hope she would retrieve anything if she ever went back to Endeh.

In the hotel in Macassar, my mother received word from Holland that her father had died; she never knew how the message had found her. Life was a see-saw, she thought; she gains her freedom, then she loses her father, and she would certainly lose all of her possessions.

After our stay at the hotel, we were moved to a house in the European section. We were there just a few days when a voice called out, "Is Mrs. Neeb here?" We were summoned to a car and were told not to ask questions. After a short ride we arrived at the airport of Macassar, where we were loaded onto a bomber, still not knowing our destination.

It turned out to be Balikpapan on the island of Borneo. Flying over it, we saw the destroyed oil fields and refineries, a scorched earth policy by the Dutch Petroleum Company as an unpleasant surprise for the Japanese invaders who had been so keen on conquering the rich oil supplies of the Dutch Indies.

We spent the night in huge hangars; many people, men and women, had already gathered on camp beds. That evening, my mother heard the aria of the Evening Star from Wagner's Tannhäuser, beautifully rendered by an American of the liberation troops. Next to Olga's piano playing in Kampili, it was the first piece of classical music she had heard in years.

At three o'clock in the morning, the three of us were fetched by jeep to go to the airport, but under the wings of the airplane, we were offered apologies that we would not be flying after all; the plane was too heavy with too much ammunition on board. We returned to our hangar in Balikpapan and waited again; a day went by, another night, then another day, accompanied by nerve-racking insecurity.

My mother struggled to keep her children entertained. That night, the same jeep came for us again, and again we wondered where we would be taken.

"You'll return to your husband," was the answer.

"But where is my husband?"

"Don't ask. Be surprised."

It was all so hush-hush that it made my mother very nervous. But she trusted that the secrecy was because of the maneuvers of my father, who had worked for our evacuation so diligently behind the scene.

Finally, we were in the air. We flew low enough that my mother could point out the beauty of the landscape underneath our plane. First, we landed in Batavia. The plane refueled and continued on to Bandung, which turned out to be our final destination, for some reason always kept secret. We were transported to a hotel, and suddenly, there was my father. He was as happily surprised as we were, we had not expected to see each other so soon. Since he had made the arrangements for our trips he knew, of course, we were coming but he had not expected that the journey would go as smoothly.

My father was in Bandung to jump-start the Pasteur Institute; to begin with, he confronted horses walking through the hallways of the building. In addition to his obligations at the Institute, he turned several schools into homes and reception centers for women and children from the camps. The three of us would be living in one of the centers until the residence he had an eye on was ready for us.

Other than his work with the Pasteur Institute, my father's instructions were to restore apothecaries and hospitals, together with a team of doctors and pharmacists. He had his hands full but did manage to procure the house for his family by kicking out the Japanese who were living there in grand style, and he organized a cleaning team. The furniture was all gone, taken by the Japs, but by buying and borrowing here and there, the place seemed sufficiently equipped to hold us all.

It was liberation for each of our family members. In September of 1945, my grandpapa still speculated where Evert, who was still missing, could be found, in which camp, in which country. He looked through every prisoners' list he could find, without any results. Then in October the devastating news of Evert's execution reached him, and the manner in which it was carried out.

Dee learned about the bombs on Hiroshima and Nagasaki and the subsequent surrender, from a woman in her prison in Semarang who spoke Japanese and could read the newspapers. Suddenly, all the guards disappeared and were replaced by Koreans. She made it home first to Batavia and then on to Bandung at the end of September by a plane belonging to RAPWI, provided by a British commander. She made sure that all the sick women in her jail could come with her to be treated at some infirmary. The pilot flew them straight to Batavia, where Dee delivered her charge at the military hospital.

To her immense surprise, one of the doctors was her own husband, Gerard. He had returned from the Burma-Thailand railroad project, and after a brief recuperation, had been put to work straight away.

Tiddy, now the widow of Evert, and her two sons Michiel and Evert-Jan came to live at one of the reception centers in Bandung. They had been transported by ambulance from their camp in Batavia by the Red Cross on orders from my father. The three of them were very sick with edema, with after-effects of dysentery and malaria and Tiddy was deaf. Because of their poor condition my father tried to get them on a troop transport to Holland as quickly as possible, but it was not until January 1946 that they finally sailed.

The house was full. My grandpapa had been released from jail, Dee had joined her small daughters who had been looked after by my grandmama, and my father, my mother, Peter, and I moved in as well. In total, nine people lived under one roof, barring the occasional visitor from a camp without a home yet. Gerard came home at the end of October when he finished his duties on the staff of the military hospital in Batavia.

My grandmama kept many animals, chickens, rabbits, geese, even a piglet. Not all of them disappeared into the frying pan. My mother assigned me the chore of cleaning up after the geese; the droppings made me feel sick, as they reminded me of the slippery latrines with the flies and smells in Kampili, but I never mentioned it. For the first time I must have sensed the presence of authority, so I did my job obediently.

The family taught us table manners, only the rudiments of it since there was not a lot of food to experiment with, but we knew not to stuff our mouths in haste or to wash our food down with big gulps of water; we understood we needed to sit straight with our elbows at our side and were shown how to use cutlery. We preferred the other way, squatting on the floor and using our fingers, but those days were over. As in the camp, we had no toys and became inventive in our play time. Peter found some safety pins and pierced them into the calluses of his feet caused by going barefoot for years in the camps. He liked the click-click on the tiles of the veranda and through the house, getting slightly on our nerves.

We looked forward to a time of peace and recuperation. However, the family had not taken into account the war of independence from the Netherlands that was raging everywhere in the Dutch East Indies.

The Japanese Empire had surrendered on August 15, 1945, and only two days later, on August 17, the nationalists under Soekarno declared the Republic of Indonesia. During the occupation, the desire for an independent Indonesia had already reared its head, which the Japanese fueled by giving young people arms and support. They had everything to gain from an unruly and weak Dutch East Indies. In 1937, Soekarno founded the Nationalist Party, subsequently he was arrested by the Dutch and imprisoned on Flores. The Japanese set him free in 1942, anticipating that the Nationalist Party would help them in the defense of the Indies in case of an attack by the Allies. The youngsters viewed Soekarno as their hero, and when he unilaterally declared the independence of Indonesia, the *pemoedas*, young men, were ready to fight.

The Bersiap had begun. Bersiap, the slogan of the boy scouts, means: "Be prepared!" It was war. For three months, anarchy, chaos, violence reigned. Ex-internees were murdered inside and outside the camps. Those internees still in the camps received protection by the British of RAPWI and, ironically, by the Japanese. The *pemoedas*, drunk with power, indiscriminately used their knives, batons, and bamboo spears and caused such bloodbaths that the Japanese advised people to stay inside the camps. Those venturing outside to look for relatives were immediately butchered.

Soekarno totally lost control of his gangs. Dutch troops finally arrived from Holland. Fighting continued for several years with many victims on both sides, the Indonesians outnumbering the other deaths by the thousands. The cause was presented to the United Nations, which resulted in a truce that did not last very long. Fighting resumed again until, finally, under pressure from America that disapproved of colonialism, the Netherlands government gave in, and the Republic of Indonesia was born in December of 1949.

We were free, but because of the Bersiap, we continued to live in a situation of war. Food was scarce; we could not get servants to help us around the house; we lived in constant fear of fires and bullets. I saw blood in our backyard and one or two figures running with drawn rifles from one end of the wall behind the house to the other. It was clearly time for my mother, Peter, and me to go to Holland, to the Vliethuis. My mother, having been so strong during the years in the camp, suffered a nervous breakdown. We had been in Bandung for ten months, partly under threatening circumstances. My father, still an army officer, continued to commute between Melbourne and Bandung.

8

Recovery

"The highest degree of a medicine is Love."
~ Paracelsus (1493–1541)

Transportation to the Netherlands of the former internees used to be effectuated by troopships, a long and uncomfortable voyage, especially trying for the weak or ill camp survivors. While my father was in Australia, he organized an airplane to take my mother, Peter, and me to Holland. It was a Super Constellation of the Dutch Indies Airline KNLM. At that time it took four days to fly from Batavia to Amsterdam-Schiphol.

My father did not join us; he would follow later, as he had to resurrect a few more ruined hospitals. We flew from Bandung to Batavia, which was our first stop on a chain of many stopovers. I was continuously airsick. The smell permeating the cabin of airplane fuel combined with the odor from the content of my little bag and the constant drone in my ears was enough for me to want to crawl under my chair and stay there.

It was a shame I was unable to hold food because, in those days, it seemed there were four-star chefs at work on the stoves in the airport kitchens. Our dinner plates were of china, our cutlery of fine steel, we had cloth napkins and a nicely printed menu, all set out on pleasant trays on a small table connected to the seat in front of us with plenty of room for our legs.

Calcutta's airport proved to be no more than an airstrip in the jungle. We spent the night in small cabins and were warned by the KNLM ground personnel to stay close to the buildings: no telling what lurked outside in the way of animals or thieves. In the airport restaurant, early in the morning, I thought I saw a spider crawling out of the wall, went out to inspect, touched it, and suffered a huge electrical shock. Pale and shaking, I went back to the breakfast table, where I faced a fried, blubbery egg. I ended up with a slice of cold toast and water. We flew on to Karachi, spent the night, and continued toward Egypt.

Somewhere in the desert near the Suez Canal was a British military camp, Adabiya. At its airport, Ataqa, we stopped for a few hours to get warm clothes for Europe, outfits that had been collected for us transit people by RAPWI. We stopped at Basra, a hot port city in Irak, and spent another night in a hotel in Cairo. We were always woken up at the oddest hours of the night; in pitch-dark, we had our breakfast. It was usually still dark when we were taken to the airport in small buses.

When we approached the Netherlands and flew at low altitude over Amsterdam to land at Schiphol Airport, the dollhouses with their red roofs, grasslands cut by rivers, the lakes and canals, the white beaches, and the ocean looked to me like pop-ups from a book I had seen at our house in Bandung.

We taxied, then the drone stopped, then the stairway was rolled out. When I stood at its top, looking down at the ground way beneath, I decided to descend sitting down. Peter followed suit. The three of us made it through all the doors and the luggage lounge. It was a cool day with a pale sun that cast shadows through the large windows of the reception hall. There stood Grandmother Waldeck; there was Frits. Hugs and tears followed and more hugs. Frits could not bear to look at us. Often, he turned away, muttering, "Oh my dear, oh my dear." I saw him fumble with a big, white piece of cloth. We must have been quite a sight.

My gaze fixed on something my grandmother wore draped around her shoulders. It had a bushy coat and beady eyes. I did not know if I should be scared, but at least it was not moving. She noticed me staring and allowed me to touch it. To my relief, it was cold and dead. "A fur stole," she explained.

We were fascinated by the ride home, tired as we were. "What are those animals? They have white and black spots."

"They are cows; they give you milk." They looked different from the cows we had seen in the camp, we never tasted their milk.

A while later: "What are those things?"

"Windmills."

"What do they do?"

"We'll take you inside someday."

It was a new world.

When we arrived, Frits honked loudly at the back gate of the house. Immediately, the door swung wide open, and barely out of the car, our three aunts swept us up into warm embraces. In the future, we would enjoy many such hugs, Peter and I always held tightly, our heads buried in silk or cotton perfumed dresses over corsets with stiff busks.

That night, in a soft bed from under fresh sheets and a light blanket, I looked into the dark beyond. I watched the shiny raindrops trickle down the rippled glass panes, illuminated by the lamp posts in the street. A long train went over the bridge, a lighted row of tiny square windows, moving by slowly enough that I could see the people inside. Where were they going? Below, in the canal, a barge chugged along steadily, the noise loud under the window. Then it faded; water of its wake splashed unto the embankment. I heard the horn. Downstairs in the living room, in my mind's eye, I saw my mother and grandmother in the light of a table lamp, and in the other living room, I imagined the aunts. I did not know why, but I cried myself to sleep.

In the Vliethuis, in the care of my grandmother and the aunts, my mother, Peter, and I would gradually recover from the damage that was done to our spirits and from the onslaught our bodies had suffered.

Vliethuis, "In de Werelt is veel Gevaer"

The family was not spared the miseries of war. A few days after the capitulation of Holland, Queen Wilhelmina and her government fled to London to continue the fight from across the canal. A raid that destroyed nearly all of The Hague had wiped out the house owned by Grandpapa and Grandmama Neeb since 1924 after my grandpapa's retirement to Holland. But the Vliethuis remained intact.

During the war, the laundry was allowed to continue its business, fuel came from the waste of the gas factory across the canal, a customized grate was installed to process cinder, coal, and dust. During the first year of the occupation, the Germans issued an incessant stream of decrees, rules, and measures. They replaced Dutch *burgomasters*, mayors, with commissars, new departments were formed, and they drew the web ever tighter.

It is fairly safe to say that the Nazi army of occupation in the Netherlands numbered nearly half a million soldiers who were paid for and fed from Dutch resources that were withheld from the general population.

In 1941, the first physical attacks against Jews occurred in Amsterdam and The Hague, causing a spontaneous strike, paralyzing public services and private institutions. The Nazis began to sense a spirit of non-cooperation by the fiercely proud Dutch, and in a speech, threatened that "whoever was not for them was against them."

It sounded ominous enough for a group to assemble and organize the Dutch resistance and sabotage units. It was a dangerous business; when caught, imprisonment, torture, and execution awaited. Saboteurs always ran the risk of betrayal. Yet, the underground movement grew and became very well structured. These groups also had in their sight the Dutch Nazis, who were collaborators, and of which there were far too many.

Food became rationed. The unrestricted and unparalleled looting and pillaging by the occupiers brought the population to the edge of starvation. Blackout rules were issued, as well as a curfew. Farmers had to export their available produce to the German Reich, with the result that what was left was either unobtainable, being used up by the Nazis, or unaffordable. Able Dutchmen, young and old, were shipped off to Germany as slave laborers to alleviate its unemployment crisis because of the departure of millions of men for the fight on the German East front and elsewhere in Europe.

The members of the Waldeck family remained safe in the Vliethuis, although their movements, like everybody else's, were sharply restricted by extended curfews and town zones that were prohibited. They shared the hunger with the rest of Holland, ate boiled or stewed tulip bulbs in the severe winter of 1944. The house was cold as the steam pipes from the laundry were not used in order to spare fuel for the business.

Grandfather Waldeck, ill with lung cancer, lost his battle a year before my mother returned home. Frits continued his dangerous work with the underground and used as his hiding place a hole he dug beneath the cellar floor of the Vliethuis.

For a while a German officer was quartered in the house, who was assigned to blow up the bridge over the canal close by. He was a decent gentleman of German aristocratic background who felt quite at home in the company of the Waldecks. He even warned the family of raids in town to catch members of the resistance, so Frits, of whose activities he indicated to be well aware, could stay safely below in the cellar. He ranked highly enough to promise Grandfather Waldeck: "Herr Graf, die Bruecke werden wir nicht sprengen," which means, "Count, we will not blow up the bridge." Living in my grandparents' home, he must have taken pity on the Dutch. The family lost track of him after he left. Even though they were grateful for his decision regarding the bridge and his protection of Frits, they had no desire to find out what had become of their officer.

In those anxious war days, the news from the Far East left no room for optimism. The worst part was the complete loss of contact. No matter how hard the family tried to find out what was happening to Oetie and her children, to Hendrik, to the Neeb family, it was all to no avail. They persistently used either the Red Cross or, through complicated detours, contacted their sources in Switzerland. The first message they received was from Hendrik after the war, that the three of us had survived the camp years and could be expected to come to Holland shortly. That "shortly," however, took nearly a year.

Immediately upon our arrival at the Vliethuis, doctors who happened to be my mother's cousins, were contacted. My father was still in the Indies and would join us a few months later. Our treatment consisted at first of lots of greens, vitamins and steel injections. When those shots made our bony buttocks black and blue, they gave us iron in the shape of pills, which upset our stomachs, as did the spoonfuls of cod liver oil.

The aunts and my grandmother supplemented our diet amply with cream, strawberries, cake, all kinds of sumptuous desserts. The domestic that had lived with the family through the war spoiled us just as much. Peter and I often had two meals a day; the aunts would invite us to join them in their dining room for their usual warm lunch at midday; my grandmother would serve dinner in the evening, which we would attend with considerable less appetite.

Both the aunts and my grandmother would set the table with white starched linen, a small vase of flowers in the center. The serving bowls were of Delft blue china, with porcelain ornaments of fruits or vegetables on the lid. Crystal knife rests on the right side of the dinner plate were used to support the sterling silver cutlery.

Next to our dish sat an array of crystal glasses, one with a flower petal in it that served as a finger bowl from which I drank, swallowing the petal, thinking it was a drinking glass for little people.

What was all this? My first world had been one of darkness, a wasteland of heat, mud, ants, flies, mess tins, slimy food. Could it be real? Would it be there again tomorrow?

We had to get used to this new world, a dangerous world without the protection of the limited surroundings we had become accustomed to in the camp. I was born with strabismus, in popular tongue a lazy eye, that could not be helped in the camp, so at long last I received a pair of glasses, which bothered me. I became accident-prone. I tripped over things, like a shoe scraper, for instance, and cut my chin; I ran into furniture; I fell over the railing of my grandmother's grand staircase, cut my eyebrow, was bleeding, howling, it required stitching, my right eyebrow shows it still. I dropped into a hole on the street, a deep one dug for electricity, I slipped by the orange warning cone. I had a car accident, unaware of the speed of the truck, and found myself lying on the pavement with long legs above me and anxious heads peering down at me. It caused a brain concussion. The next concussion occurred on the playing ground when I did not see a swing, it hit the side of my head, poor Peter saw it all and was helpless and horrified; the scar is still there. Then there were the pipes. I did not understand what the steaming pipes were for, I sat on one of them near the tub in the bathroom; my skin stuck to it.

*Hulda and Peter recovering in the Vliethuis with the doll
my father had brought from Australia*

Each time, the aunts or my grandmother comforted me with hugs, with more cream, more strawberries, more desserts. They lavished care and attention on us the same way they loved Frits and my mother when they were young. I did not know how old the aunts were; they were of my grandparents' generation. I keep their portraits, made in the days of our recuperation, on my dressing table.

They are my angels.

The aunts, from left to right, Jette, Louise, and Kaethe in Jette's bedroom

The aunts welcomed Peter and me into their respective bedrooms. One day, it was in Kaethe's room, one day in Louise's, or another day in Jette's room, large rooms with shining parquet floors. We would run, catch a rug, and sail to the other end. The aunts, in bed, would be covered by fluffy eiderdowns, and to this day, I don't know who enjoyed these visits more. I still have a letter written by Kaethe in 1958, in which she says she wished she could have expressed her love for us better. She, nor Louise or Jette, have any idea how they restored our spirits, how instrumental they were in our recovery.

They let us use the fabulous gong in the hallway if there was a message to be given to a member of the household. Often, they sat with us on the lawn, showing us ladybugs while braiding daisies.

"Daisies die," they said, "but they come back the next year." Peter had more pressing things on his mind. "When I die, do my bowels also go the heaven?" He knew a thing or two about his anatomy after the camp years and clearly hoped to stay in one piece.

The Christmas holidays were pure magic, the house filled with the aromas of pine needles, of baked goods, of lighted candles. The secrecy surrounding the wrapping of gifts with doors quickly shut when we children approached added to our excitement.

My grandmother gave me another great gift. One day, she was tired; she ran out of steam controlling her wild grandchildren, who were loud and untamed. She called us into her living room, and once more, asked us to quiet down. Her recourse was always her love of music. From a drawer in her low antique cabinet, she retrieved a record; I watched her use the mechanism of a heavy ball on a steel arm, put the contraption on a disc, and there came the sounds.

I sat close to her; we listened together. She explained to me that it was a piano, and she mentioned the name Mozart. I had seen a piano in the camp but not heard it played like this and, above all, played together with so many more musical instruments. From here on until we returned to Batavia in December of 1948, my grandmother and I listened to music together whenever we had the opportunity. The aunts had a big Grundig radio in their living room with touch keys for the channels. They allowed me to sit behind it, and I pretended to be a concert pianist. My mother's piano was gone by then.

Commodities were rationed. Because we had been in a concentration camp, the number of our ration stamps was increased, as for instance, the stamps for toilet paper. Peter and I were sent to the store, each with a long piece of string and told to come home with as many rolls as it could hold. We obliged and draped the string around our shoulder, but I remember how tired we were. We were always tired, but this time, even more so, burdened with our charge. We squatted on the curb of the street, the local Indies' way, a habit my grandmother tried time and again to correct, but out of reach, we automatically sat on our heels to rest up before heading back.

To our delight, a street organ-grinder came by with a monkey, grinding out music which I later in life recognized as melodies from Bellini's Norma, Donizetti's Lucia, Verdi's Nabucco. We returned to the Vliethuis out of breath with excitement.

Michiel's homecoming was a different one. His grandparents' house was not large. Tiddy, Michiel, and Evert-Jan had a remodeled attic at their disposal, the only ornament a full armor of a medieval knight in the corner that scared Michiel. Not much sunlight came through. Evert-Jan decided to emigrate to Australia; he was about seventeen years old and seeking adventure. The attic was a little too tight for him.

Michiel, Peter, and I went to school together. We used to walk by a ditch, and one day, to my horror, Michiel caught a frog and tore it apart, blood, bones and all. I was determined not to share the walk by the ditch with him anymore and always crossed the street before we got there.

On April 17, 1948, Easter Sunday, my father called us out of bed early in the morning.

"Come with me; I have a surprise for you."

Peter and I were delighted, "Are we going to have an extra egg?" Even with the hunger pangs now several years in the past, the prospect of an extra egg still held its charm.

We were taken upstairs to a cradle; in it was Robbert. "Where did he come from?" we wanted to know. "I'll tell you later," said my mother.

Our recovery continued. We were fed, nursed, hugged. Security surrounded us; we lived in a healing environment.

The benefits of food were explained to us. In the aunties' kitchen, we watched the preparations on our own stools. To our delight, tasting was part of our education. We liked school and especially the class with the strange Bible stories of camels and kings and people in long robes near wells and funny trees. The family looked forward to the times we had our class; they enjoyed hearing how we had processed the stories. Our interpretations amused them endlessly. Egyptian dynasties were confusing, "Because the viceroy is lower than the king, he lives downstairs; the real king lives upstairs."

We found learning to read and write great adventures, the inkwell at our desk a curiosity. From the big book of the fairy tales by the brothers Grimm my mother read us bedtime stories, it was an unfailing routine; my father took us for walks along the canal. My mother was also recuperating, and towards the end of 1948, she felt well and rested enough to return with us to Batavia. My father took additional courses in internal medicine and tropical diseases at Leyden University. In May he returned ahead of us to the Indies since several clinics were awaiting his touch again to be reopened. In the meantime, he left the army and returned to civilian life.

My mother, Peter, and Hulda well recovered in Holland, 1947

9

Return to Batavia

"If I am to meet with a disappointment, the sooner I know it,
the more of life I shall have to wear it off."
~ Thomas Jefferson (1743–1826)

Air travel had improved in the two years since our flight from Bandung in 1946; the return trip was considerably shorter. My mother, Peter and I left Holland in December of 1948.

In Batavia, we moved into a fairly comfortable house with a nice terrace, surrounded by a garden. The road was split by a shallow *kali*, canal, of red, muddy water. The friends we would make lived across the street from us.

For a year, life was pleasant enough, but the Dutch Indies my father had hoped to find again was gone, even though he should have known better, as he had seen the beginning of the conflict when we lived in Bandung. The fight for independence, the Bersiap, that had started under the leadership of Soekarno, was still going on in parts of the country. Dutch troops arrived from Holland, one detachment in 1946, another one in 1947, and the last one in 1948. In the meantime, deliberations continued between Soekarno's Nationalists, the Dutch government, and the United Nations.

Peter and I went to school, too far to walk, and were taken by *betjah*, an open two-seater sometimes covered with a tarp, pulled by a coolie on a bicycle. My parents had no concerns about our safety. We enjoyed our adventurous rides on busy streets with noisy cars, other *betjahs*, and many bicycles. At home, we had our *kokkie*, our *kebon*, our *babu*, like we had in Endeh. Peter and I shared a room in the front of the house, Robbert had the room between ours and our parents' bedroom. The house had the typical layout of a tropical bungalow.

Peter, Robbert, and Hulda on our garden wall

In 1949, Grandpapa and Grandmama Neeb visited us on their way to Holland; they had decided to leave Bandung, disillusioned; these were not the Indies of old, the war had brought the end of an era. Life had become very dangerous, and the future was uncertain. Besides, my grandparents needed medical attention. My grand-mama's eyesight was seriously failing, due to a continued deficiency of vitamins during the war, and many more ailments surfaced. Dee, Gerard, and the girls were also making preparations to leave.

The family, Hans not born yet, in Batavia in 1949

On December 27, 1949, the Dutch East Indies received their independence from the Netherlands government and became the Republic of Indonesia with Soekarno as president, Batavia baptized as Jakarta. Festivities made it a loud and noisy day, with bobbing masses of jubilant Indonesians all over the city. It was best to stay close to home.

After the transfer of sovereignty, circumstances deteriorated. We were obliged to cut our rupiahs in two, with the promise that bonds would be issued, which never happened. The new government literally confiscated our money.

My mother sold linens, jewelry, and silver on the black market to buy food. We did away with the car, and my father went to work on a bicycle. Now it became unsafe for Peter and me to go to school in the *betjah*. Trucks picked up all the children in the neighborhood to drive us to our classes under the protection of Dutch troops.

Robberies and assaults were the routines of the day. Peter and I had some scary moments when, at night, we noticed shadows peering into our room. We would become very still, stop talking, practically stop breathing. Thieves roamed around our house, and my father hired a night watch. It began to dawn on my parents that perhaps we should also return to Holland. For my father, this was a bitter pill. The tropics, the old Dutch East Indies, were in his blood. With sorrow he witnessed the crumbling of an era, the memories of old trampled upon. He aimed at a career comparable to what his uncles had accomplished, but for this goal, he needed a country that would accommodate him, not a country that was becoming more and more hostile. When in Bandung, at war's end, he showed he had the talent, vision, and stamina that were very much on display in his father and uncles. The Dutch government amply decorated him for his efforts. But the changes brought on in Indonesia by its independence and the ensuing animosity toward the erstwhile mother country, upset his plans entirely. Whether he liked it or not, he had to arrive at the conclusion that this was not the environment he had envisioned for a worthy career or a land he would enjoy spending his life or exposing his family to.

My brother Hans was born in May of 1950. We still were not told where this child after Robbert had suddenly come from, but here he was, another member of the family. We, the children, enjoyed a carefree existence. There was something to say for life in the tropics. We got rid of all the heavy clothes we had to wear in Holland. The ride to school at first in the *betjah*, later by truck, was exciting. It did not matter that we got soaked in the rainstorms of the wet monsoon. We got paid a few cents for collecting the snails, emerging after each downpour that were destroying the plants. We did not care for the job, but the money was good. Vendors came by the house with their wares either on a *picul*, which was a stick over the shoulder with at each end a box on a string, or strapped in crates on the backseat of their bicycles. We bought sticky lemonade with our snail money, and sometimes for dinner at dusk, my father would hail a coolie to prepare a dish in front of us on his glowing coal stove. We had friends; we invented our toys and our games; life was simple and structured.

Not so for our parents. When my mother ran out of items to sell on the market for our bare necessities, my father began to look around for transportation to return to Holland.

We struggled on until the end of September 1950.

Since we had no money in Indonesia, the only way we could afford passage was on a freight ship with passenger accommodation, my father employed as its physician, and so the journey could be free. My father located a British ship, the *Ormonde*, that would convey us back home to safety. Our quarters were cramped, the six of us stayed in a narrow cabin. As I was violently ill with seasickness most of the time, my father regularly fed me salt and water and took me up on the deck on a swing he had improvised to push me counter to the movement of the ship. My parents almost lost me on this voyage.

We enjoyed the excitement of passing slowly through the Suez Canal, halting once for exotic merchants in small boats coming close to the ship. I saw the desert, the camels, the palm trees, and concluded they were real, not just drawings in a book. Robbert disappeared from the cabin one day; the window was open. After a frantic search by the ship's crew and us, he was found below deck, wandering around in his diapers just before the captain was considering to reverse course.

After a journey of three weeks, we docked at the port of Rotterdam.

For the second time, we arrived at the Vliethuis destitute, exhausted and in need of a home. Once again, we were received with open arms.

The future was questionable, but my parents were confident that once we were healthy again, we would find our way.

Afterword

O n the face of it, one could say that everything returned to some
kind of normality at the end of the war. The days became weeks,
and months, and years. But we, camp survivors, would for quite some
time live on a volcano of frustrations and unprocessed emotions. For
the most part, the deprivations had destroyed our health. To us
youngsters, thrown into the camp as toddlers or very young children,
the world after the camp was totally alien, at times exciting, at times
scary. The camp was a wasteland in one way; outside the camp, the
rubble of ruined towns made for a different type of wasteland.

Nothing was easy to obtain; Hitler put his stamp and his boots
on Europe. Cities lay in ruins; food and household necessities were
rationed, and in some cases, entirely unavailable for a while. The
world was still not a safe place. During the war years, the ground was
laid for revenge. Hatred and loyalties had shifted, murderous actions
continued, and fierce battles would be fought all over Asia and in
Europe until the rage was finally spent.

On a smaller scale, collaborators in each country were rounded
up, and the cruelest means of punishment would be meted out to the
poor wretches before a jeering crowd.

The advent of the Marshall Plan contributed in a large measure
to the stabilization of life. Concerns about the spread of Communism
weighed heavily on Europe at the end of World War II, the root of it
being economic discontent.

The American secretary of state, George Marshall, brought forth
a plan for the nations of Europe, including Russia, to rebuild and

reform their economies. From 1946 to 1952, the United States Treasury loaned $16 million, at that time a huge amount of money, to seventeen European countries, including the Netherlands and Germany. The major cooperation between regions also worked to enlarge markets, and industries and agriculture could expand. This, again, served as a great advantage to the United States, which was looking at future trade deals.

The Marshall Plan stabilized society throughout free Europe, and thus frustrated the Communist expectations of an imminent collapse. Through the plan, consumption goods began to reappear. This brought hope, perhaps even some cheer, and an incentive to pick up the broken pieces.

But for the survivors, the saddest part of the much-anticipated return was the surprising ignorance they met on the home front. It stemmed from the total absence of any communications with Southeast Asia during the war years that led to questions like: "Why did you not escape? Why are you so thin? Why did your mother not take better care of you? Where was your father?" Comments similar to: "We had our own terrible war; we don't want any more war stories," were not unusual. We were obviously not welcome, the authorities, as well as a large part of the Dutch population were hostile. It was conveniently forgotten how much the country had benefitted from the former colonies, either culturally or economically.

More insults came our way: "You are despicable colonialists." "It was warm over there. We had cold winters." "Your soils were fertile so food would grow. We had to eat flower bulbs in the Hunger Winter."

This attitude was accompanied by an astonishing lack of understanding of the far-reaching damage that had been done to the bodies and souls of their relatives, of their friends.

It was a very cold shower.

Not for one or two years was it recognized that many of the survivors were afflicted with a concentration camp syndrome, which today we would call post-traumatic stress disorder or PTSD. These patients, young and old, were haunted by nightmares, anxiety attacks, insomnia, depression. Their chances for a happy life were minimal.

Professor Bastiaans of the Leyden University conducted pioneering work in the field of the camp syndrome, although his methods, and he himself, became very controversial. He treated his patients with LSD, in order to make them relive the past. His theory was that a trauma in the open could be treated more effectively than encapsulated trauma.

Yet, through his activities that put the spotlight onto the problem, various projects were established to promote studies and expertise with special training facilities. My brother Peter sat on the board of the government foundation Het Gebaar, gebaar (gesture), established in 2001, a gesture meant to deal with the criticism of the unjust treatment of the returnees from the Dutch East Indies and in support of subsidies from the Dutch government.

The foundation managed, within one year, to trace approximately 100,000 Dutch citizens spread over Holland and the diaspora in America, Australia, South Africa, New Zealand, and in other countries, who were eligible for monetary compensation. Speed was of the essence, as many beneficiaries were aging or in ill-health. Psychiatrists, psychologists, or for that matter, any type of care provider, did not know enough about the East Indies Concentration Camp Syndrome. The older generation was particularly affected; they would either talk incessantly about their experiences or remain totally silent. One way or another, their behavior reflected badly on the children, and as a result, their offspring and even the third generation continued to suffer to some degree.

Besides supporting research centers, the foundation ensured the availability of funds, as well as a small compensation that we, victims, received a few years later in 2002. It was no more than a gesture, the foundation stipulated, because the honest and real redress should come from the Japanese government, a government that to this day avoids the moral issues and denies the brutal strategies of the Imperial Army. A few Japanese prime ministers have issued some kind of an apology; however, it comes too late and is too little. No history books in schools mention the Japanese aggression.

Another foundation established in 1990, the Foundation of Japanese Honorary Debts, endeavors to make the Japanese government pay its war victims an amount of $20,000 per individual. So far it has not paid us any money, nor has it admitted any guilt. It appears that Japan is determined to wait until the last of us has died.

Nevertheless, the foundation continues its dialogue with the Japanese government through, among other things, delivering a petition to the Japanese ambassador once a month and with demonstrations in front of the embassy in The Hague. The Germans have paid their victims billions in compensation and reparations, and America has done likewise for the Nissei; though if not with a comparable amount, it was still a compensation. Also, Australia, New Zealand, and Great Britain compensated losses sustained in the conflict and did so generously and in proper time.

The war past continues to be very much alive in the Netherlands and is duly remembered. Apart from the earlier mentioned foundations, every year on August 15, a solemn commemoration takes place nationwide at several monuments to war victims of the Dutch East Indies, organized by the National Commemoration 15 August 1945 Foundation. The main event occurs in The Hague, every five years in the presence of the king, but each year the Dutch prime minister and other dignitaries, the Diplomatic Corps, and representatives of the Allied forces attend.

Peter sits on this advisory board as well. The foundation also strives to educate young people by informing them about the events that led to the war in the former colony and in Southeast Asia. Special youth groups were established with the objective of making the younger generation familiar with the facts of the little-known war, encouraging them to study the tragedies and triumphs of World War II.

Also, every year, in the evening of May 4, the day before Holland was liberated in 1945, a commemoration of the victims of Nazi-Germany in Holland and the European theater takes place. The king and queen, together with representatives of the government, hold a silent and solemn ceremony with wreaths and "the Last Post", taps, on a trumpet at the site of the National Monument in the main square across from the palace in Amsterdam.

There was no joy in the homecoming of Tiddy, Evert-Jan, and Michiel. Other than meeting with the total incomprehension in Holland regarding the sufferings of Japanese captives, the trauma of the decapitation of husband and father was practically insurmountable. For some time, until they had found adequate lodgings, they lived in Voorburg, as we did, in the attic of Tiddy's parental home, the knight in full armor in the corner making Michiel uncomfortable. Tiddy developed the art of lip-reading and Evert-Jan left for Australia, where he did well as a partner in a house-painting firm. He married the owner's daughter. He liked champagne, lots of it, and died of a heart attack in 2007. He had no children.

Tiddy never talked to Michiel about the past or his father. The subject was taboo. Michiel's frustrations grew more and more intense, and so it was decided to subject him to Professor Bastiaans' LSD treatment, the hopes high that his nightmares, depression, and headaches would disappear. It did not happen; if anything, he looked his past straight in the face, resulting in a panoply of psychoses. His life was not a happy one. He married, had a son, divorced, and had many jobs until he received disability benefits from the state. In May of 2017, he finally gave up. He ingested some Chinese concoction, went to sleep, and did not wake up.

He had committed suicide.

Against this backdrop, the compassionate determination my mother, Peter, and I encountered from the women at the Vliethuis, my grandmother, the three aunts, and the domestic, Nell, to heal us, was nothing more nor less than a godsend. We were given our own rooms in the house and the much-needed privacy we had not known for many years. Our ailments, physical and emotional, were understood and taken care of. It is in the Vliethuis where our regeneration began. In later days, Peter and I would say that without the care in those postwar years of the women in that magic house, we did not think we could have grown up with sound minds and bodies. They put us back on our feet, and in the meantime, taught us a lesson in compassion and generosity.

In 1950, when we returned tired and penniless again from Indonesia, the family picked up their care for us where they had left off in 1948. We lived under the protection of the Vliethuis until we were strong enough to face the world and new challenges.

My grandmother and I began to listen to music again on a regular basis. By then, she allowed me to select my own records from the magical drawer and start up the gramophone. My mother often joined us. Did both my mother and my grandmother know about the healing powers of music? Or was it by sheer intuition that they were aware of it? Ever since those wondrous days of listening to Mozart, Bach, Schubert, to sopranos, violins, pianos, classical music became my steady companion and comfort.

When Grandpapa and Grandmama Neeb returned to Holland, they settled with their daughter, Dee; son-in-law, Gerard; and their granddaughters, Lily and Edith, in The Hague. My grandmama was forever homesick for the Indies of her past. Often, she would go shopping in a street with small Indonesian restaurants, enjoying long chats with the owners and always returning home with the most delectable tidbits. I remember those from the time we visited with our grandparents. I can still taste them.

My father, Hendrik (Henk) Neeb

My father moved the family from Voorburg to Arnhem. He joined the staff of one of the hospitals and started his practice in internal medicine with a specialty in tropical diseases. But the tropics continued to pull at him, and in 1953, he moved to Dutch New Guinea, along with my mother, Robbert, and Hans. Peter and I stayed behind in our house with a guardian to finish school. The family lived in Ifar, a small mountain town, in a quonset house that was once the R and R for General Douglas McArthur and his staff while they were in

Hollandia at New Guinea's coast during the war. Peter and I spent our holidays in Ifar.

House in Ifar, Dutch New-Guinea

The relationship between our father and his eldest children did not quite get off the ground. He provided well for the family, but the affection and closeness Peter and I had developed with our mother never equaled the feelings we had for him. After all, during the first years of our life, it was our mother who protected Peter and me, comforted us, kept us from dying of sickness and malnutrition. At the end of the war, her desire to heal us expressed itself among many things in her determination to leave the camp years behind her; she would not allow the dark years to become part of our lives.

But I knew she was hurting when she fainted coming upon a group of Japanese tourists in a museum we visited. She hardly ever mentioned our imprisonment until much later when I asked her about our past.

Yearly, Kampili survivors put together a reunion, which my mother chose never to attend. "To remember the good old days?"

Sadly, in 1964, our parents divorced. Could it be that their marriage was another victim of the war? For several years, they were involuntarily separated when they had just been married. My mother had her specific experiences in the concentration camp; my father had his life in Australia and the Pacific, their respective courses necessarily divergent. They had two more children, my brothers Robbert and Hans, but since in those days divorce was not socially acceptable, they may have struggled on for many years. We, the children, were unaware of any tensions. They both remarried.

After my graduation, I went on to study languages, starting at the interpreter school in Geneva, continuing in Munich. In 1963, I joined the Dutch Foreign Service until 1996. Over the course of these years, the Ministry of Foreign Affairs posted me at our embassies in twenty-five countries. On the way, I met and married Jim, a historian who relinquished his teaching job in the United States to join me on my assignments. I met Jim through a friend.

Hulda at a ceremony to be introduced to the president of India

One of my jobs took me to our Embassy in New Delhi. I stayed at a nice hotel, and one fine day, I heard a Scarlatti sonata coming from the bar that had only produced a medley of Strauss waltzes so far. I checked, and there was an American gentleman at the piano, part of a group of National Geographic photographers that was preparing for an expedition to Nepal. He was a friend of Jim's and returned to the United States with a message for him, a bachelor: "I have met your wife. She likes Mozart." He insisted Jim write to me, which he did, reluctantly, since all throughout their friendship David had been trying to set him up on blind dates.

We continued to write, we met in Holland when I had finished my task at the embassy, I returned with Jim to the United States, and in 1987, we were married in New York. I continued my employment with the Dutch Foreign Service, now with Jim by my side.

But at some junction, both of us grew tired of lugging suitcases all over the world, adjusting to hotels or rented apartments, no matter how exotic the countries were that we visited, and so we decided to hang it up. We restored a Pre-Civil War house in Virginia but wanted to move to the Midwest, Jim's origins. We opted for Estes Park, which my husband had known as a young man, hiking in the Rockies on vacation from Nebraska.

Peter continued his studies in economics and returned to Jakarta, to join an import-export firm for a few years. After that, in the early 1970s, he worked in Kabul, Afghanistan, as an international trader, combining it with the position of honorary vice-consul for the Netherlands, Belgium, and Luxemburg, the BeNeLux, countries that were not represented by embassies.

However, he decided he liked politics better and continued his career as a member of several government institutions and political parties. He was elected *burgomaster*, mayor, of Zundert and of Oudenbosch. Zundert, incidentally, is the birthplace of the Dutch painter Vincent van Gogh. Both towns were among the first ones liberated in October and November of 1944 by the "Timberwolves," who stood among the very first American divisions to land on Dutch soil.

Since the whole of the Netherlands was not free until May of 1945, it shows the long and fierce battles the Allies were destined to fight to conquer the Germans in such a relatively small country. As veterans of World War II, the Timberwolves often visited their old battlegrounds, warmly received by welcoming committees and honored with dinners and receptions. When the area became the center of rapid industrial and technological development, right now it is practically the Silicon Valley of Europe, Queen Beatrix paid a visit to Oudenbosch.

Queen Beatrix with Peter Neeb, Burgomaster, in center, wearing his chain of office, and the Provincial Governor, Frank Houben

Peter continued as burgomaster of two more towns and finally retired. He married Alja and has a son and a daughter, and now three grandchildren.

He toured Indonesia with his family once or twice, and on one of his visits, he returned to the island of our birth. He tried to locate our house in Endeh, but it had been demolished. He did visit the jetty where my father departed on the schooner for Australia and said goodbye to my mother and her toddlers.

The aunties died, first Jette, then Louise, and lastly Kaethe. Each time, I mourned their passing; each time, I reflected on their invaluable contribution to our recovery.

The Vliethuis became emptier. I visited with my grandmother as often as I could. After Frits lost his wife, he moved in to take care of my grandmother, who was ailing. When she passed away, my mother and Frits decided to sell the house and the laundry business. A building company bought the property with the intention to convert it into several apartments. Strangely enough, soon after the purchase, the attic caught fire; the new owner was suspected of insurance fraud.

The house changed hands again, and finally, the construction of the apartments began. It kept its name, "In de Werelt is veel Gevaer." I have walked by the house a few times, but it was painful to glance through a window and discover that my grandmother's precious marble-floored kitchen was now serving as an entrance hall with doorbells and mailboxes. I shudder to think about what was done to the rest of the house.

The generation that led us out of the corruption and the savagery visited upon us has now totally departed the stage. Our elders guided us, taught us the basics of civilization, and set a pattern of values and behavior.

Peter and I, and the men and women of our age who came out of war and destitution, are fully aware of the costs incurred by our predecessors in reestablishing a world of order and prosperity.

Our parents and grandparents have our gratitude forever. The freedom they created for us, we treasure and protect.

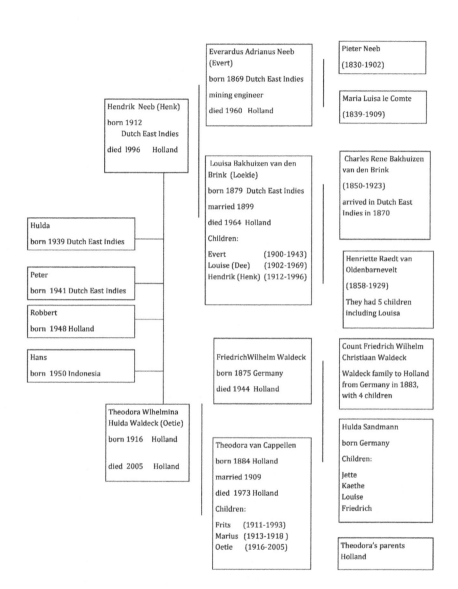

Abbreviated Family Tree

Selected Bibliography

Buruma, Ian. *Year Zero, a History of 1945.* The Penguin Press, New York, 2013.

Chang, Iris. *The Rape of Nankin, the forgotten Holocaust of WWII.* Penguin Books, New York, 1997.

Colijn, Helen. *Song of Survival, Women interned; a true story which inspired the motion picture "Paradise Road."* White Cloud Press, Ashland, Oregon, 1995.

Daws, Gavan. *Prisoners of the Japanese, POWs of World War II in the Pacific.* Quill William Morrow, New York, 1994.

Deibler Rose, Darlene. *Evidence not seen, a Woman's Miraculous Faith in the Jungles of World War II.* Harper One, New York, 1988.

Fenton Huie, Shirley. *The Forgotten Ones, Women and Children Under Nippon.* Angus and Robertson, Pymble, Australia, 1993.

Herman, Arthur. *Freedom's Forge, How American Business Produced Victory in World War II.* Random House Trade Paperback, New York, 2013

Mac Arthur, Brian. *Surviving the Sword, Prisoners of the Japanese in the Far East 1942–1945.* Random House, New York, 2005.

Manchester, William. *American Caesar, Douglas MacArthur, 1880–1964.* Little, Brown and Company, Boston, 1998.

Motley, John L. *The Life and Death of John of Barneveld, Advocate of Holland.* Harper and Brothers, New York, 1874.

Newton Keith, Agnes. *Three came Home*. Little, Brown and Company, in Association with the Atlantic Monthly Press, Book-of-the-Month Club, New York, 1946.

Roberts, Andrew. *The Storm of War, a new History of the Second World War*. Harper Collins, New York, 2011.

Russell, Edward F.L *The Knights of Bushido, a History of Japanese War Crimes during World War II*. Skyhorse Publishing, Delaware, 2008.

Schama, Simon. *The Embarrassment of Riches, an Interpretation of Dutch Culture in the Golden Age*. University of California Press, Berkeley, 1988.

Schulman, Andrew. *Waking the Spirit, a Musician's Journey healing Body, Mind, and Soul*. Picador, New York, 2016.

Thompson-Gray, John. *Love, Luck and Larceny, Memoirs from Broome 1942*. John Thompson-Gray Pty Ltd, 2015.

Van Velden, D. *De Japanse Burgerkampen, with English Appendix*. Wever BV, Franeker, Holland, 1985.

Acknowledgments

Since our move to Estes Park in 2002, my husband, James Bachman, a professional historian, and I have met with many requests to give public presentations about events during World War II, and the experiences of myself and my family.

The public's intense interest shown at these talks, and its curiosity about the subject matter, finally persuaded me to commit my story to book form.

When preparing the presentations and while writing this book, Jim has been, and always will be, a pillar of strength and my refuge. I can't thank him enough for his patience and understanding.

My brother Peter Neeb, as the keeper of the family archives, has been very cooperative in providing me with documentary sources. Because he is domiciled in the Netherlands, our contacts were predominantly by e-mail. It was of great help that he always answered my requests for additional information promptly. This book is as much Peter's story as it is mine, and his unwavering support and input assisted me considerably in moving it along.

My friends Audrey and Mack Hunt asked me to talk about the values of freedom and the effects of the loss of it at a Fourth of July Celebration in Estes Park. "The story needs to be told," they insisted. This was fifteen years ago. Audrey and Mack got the ball rolling, with the result that Jim and I have given well over twenty presentations in and around Estes Park and the Valley.

Several years ago, an extensive family chronicle was composed by my cousin Edith Moens-Kloosterhuis for the benefit of her children, grandchildren, and relatives. Her manuscript gives an in-depth overview of our history. I am grateful that I had her writings at my disposal.

My nephew Jeffrey Buehner gave me a fair amount of his precious time touching up historical photographs on the computer, for which I am very grateful. To me, the task resembled a labyrinth from which Jeff rescued me.

The direction and technical expertise of my dedicated friend Carol Kirkstadt have been invaluable. She was always available to answer any requests for help and never failed to encourage me when the going got tough.

Maggie Treadway tried to procure a better copy of the press release of April 1942, contacting her friends in Perth, Australia. It turned out that the result was identical to the clipping my family owns. We thank her for her kind efforts.

Nick Zelinger designed an artistic cover for my book. He was also instrumental in its production, turning the many pages of my manuscript into a worthy interior. His creativity was inspirational, as was his know-how. While my book was in the making, he was always ready to give advice.

Nick introduced me to his daughter Jen Zelinger, an editor by profession, whose impressive skills were on full display when she scrutinized my text word for word. I am very thankful for her intelligent support, her cheerfulness, and her belief in my endeavor.

Last, but not least, I am especially appreciative of my friends at my Bible study class. Their prayers and encouragement have sustained me all through this process, beginning with the presentations many years ago. From my heart, a big thank you goes to Bonnie, Cheryl, Claire, Dodi, Jeanne, Joy, Linda, Lois, Marna, Nan, Pam, Pat M., Patti D., Ruth, Sharon, Tina, and to all those ladies who have since moved away.

Estes Park, Colorado
Summer 2019

About the Author

Hulda Bachman–Neeb was born in Indonesia of colonial Dutch parentage two years before the Pearl Harbor attack on December 7, 1941. Because much of Asia fell under Japanese control, all non-Asians were imprisoned in concentration camps until August of 1945, the end of the war in the Pacific.

As a member of the Dutch Foreign Service in her adult life, Hulda held assignments in twenty-five countries over a period of thirty-six years, retiring in 1996.

She is married to an American, James Bachman, a historian and author, and has dual citizenship.

Hulda and her husband live in Estes Park, Colorado.